Anxious Attachment Recovery

How to Self-Soothe, Regulate Your Emotions, Build Intimate Relationships and Overcome Abandonment Anxiety

Alison Bishop

Table of Contents

Introduction 4

Chapter 1: What Is Attachment? 7

Chapter 2: The Attachment Styles 10

Chapter 3: What Is Anxious Attachment? 18

Chapter 4: Signs of Someone With Anxious Attachment 21

Chapter 5: Why Do We Fall Into Anxious Attachment? 24

Chapter 6: How to Deal and Cope With Your Anxious Attachment Style ? ... 27

Chapter 7: Signs of an Anxious Attachment in a Relationship 34

Chapter 8: The Effects of Anxious Attachment on Romantic Relationships . 38

Chapter 9: Cultivate the Relationship You Have and Strengthen the Feeling of Security 49

Chapter 10: The Ultimate Dating Exercises 53

Chapter 11: The Effects of Anxious Attachment on Professional Relationships 62

Chapter 12: Steps to Strive Toward Secure Attachment Style 66

Chapter 13: Acknowledging Your Anxious Attachment 76

Chapter 14: Understanding My Triggers 86

Chapter 15: Learn to Let Go of Your Anxious Attachment 92

Chapter 16: Overcoming Negative Interactions 99

Chapter 17: Improve Your Self-Confidence and Self-Esteem 103

Chapter 18: Reforming Your Attachment Style 112

Chapter 19: Envisioning the Future 124

Conclusion 128

Author's Note 131

Introduction

D o you feel like you constantly fear that you will lose your partner? Do you frequently worry about their whereabouts when they are not by your side? Do you feel like your partner only pays attention to you when they need advice about how to improve their life? If this sounds similar, there is a significant probability that one or both partners have an anxious attachment style.

It is not unusual for a secure person to marry an anxious person, and fifteen years later, begin experiencing panic attacks. It is also possible that you felt anxious when you first started dating your partner but believed that things would improve after you had kids and/or started living together. It is only now that you start to consider whether this might be a recurring issue.

Nevertheless, perhaps your history is more along the lines of this: You were the anxious person in the relationship because you lacked the confidence to let others get close to you. Because it seemed inevitable that they would reject you, you dated other anxious people. But, they did not. And you reasoned that perhaps they could educate you on how to quit being so clingy. But, ten or fifteen years later, they are still carrying out the things they were doing at the beginning. You are, too.

And perhaps now, your partner is saying things like, "You are being overly sensitive," "You are making me feel guilty," or "Just calm down. It is not that awful." Or perhaps they believe that you are in denial about how bad things are. Or maybe they are confused as to why they cannot simply get more of what they want.

Your partner's anxiety may be preventing you from fully enjoying the quality of your relationship since you do not feel secure enough to talk to them or give them your full attention. And if your love relationship is not going very well, you can experience a similar scenario in your other relationships.

Anxious attachment relationships have their positive and negative aspects, just like any other type of relationship. When your partner is not anxious, there may be many amazing things about how they behave; conversely, there may be many extremely annoying things about how they behave when they are anxious. Of course, there may be times when you will be angry with your partner for something they have done and express your anger to them. This can feel like a significant step forward when you do it. Nevertheless, it can also trigger a variety of resentments; you might get the impression that they are just being defensive, do not truly understand what you are saying, or are taking it too personally.

And if that rings a bell in your relationship, things may not be going well. Yet you are not the only one at fault. Your partner may be experiencing anxiety, which could explain how they are behaving.

How do you stop acting in ways that make you anxious and stop feeling insecure? What should you do if your partner needs help but is unwilling to ask for it?

Even if you might not be treating your partner's problems seriously enough, it is equally possible that they are. Because their anxiety is a result of past trauma, they might not be able to manage it. Your relationship might develop in a new and very positive way if you can figure out a means to deal with these anxiety triggers together. Yet there is a significant probability that your relationship will continue to suffer if you cannot communicate with each other in a way that makes dealing with these problems simpler.

But, it is also possible that you are experiencing anxiety in the same way as they are but are simply unaware of it. If so, you might not even be aware that you are acting like an anxious attachment partner. The situation will not improve if you are not even aware of it. Yet, if you accept this and seek out help for yourself, your relationship may progress.

It is not always simple to support your partner through their anxieties. They could find talking about their issues to be quite uncomfortable. And this might result in defense mechanisms like rage, denial, and increased effort to make their anxiety go away on their own. It is crucial that you keep trying and reaching out, even if it is difficult at first, for the benefit of both parties. Continue reading if you want to learn how to handle your anxious relationship.

Some individuals are quite insecure, but if they feel they can find an anxious partner, they may decide that this will be sufficient to improve their self-esteem. Some could determine that although having an anxious partner will be difficult, doing so will make their lives more meaningful. It is crucial to keep in mind that being in an anxious relationship is not necessarily a bad thing. It can be among the nicest things that have ever occurred to you because it can make managing your anxiety easier. It might even provide you with the motivation you need to manage your anxiety.

Chapter 1:
What Is Attachment?

John Bowlby's Attachment Theory

The term "attachment" refers to a strong and long-lasting emotional bond between two individuals.

John Bowlby is one of the founding figures of attachment theory and is often considered its father. His theories and findings served as the foundation for additional research into how our interactions with others are influenced by our past experiences, particularly with our primary caregivers.

The idea that people are "wired for intimacy" naturally is a part of Bowlby's theory. He meant by this that our drive to make strong ties with other people is something we biologically develop from birth. An infant or toddler is instructed to seek proximity to their caregiver when in distress and to maintain contact during moments of comfort and security through the attachment system, a fundamental emotion-driven behavioral mechanism. The framework for developing relationships and our expectations of others is set by the attachment system, which remains with us well into adulthood.

The idea of attachment is also connected to evolution, according to Bowlby, who claims that attachment is a survival mechanism our ancestors implemented for their descendants to secure their safety and survival. Bowlby's theories on attachment are based on his observations of young children who had to be separated from their primary caregiver due to adoption or death. He looked at their coping mechanisms and environmental adjustments. He also examined kids who had caregiver absences, including parents who were regularly gone for business or other reasons. In all of his observations, Bowlby found that the child-caregiver bond and attachment were the most crucial factors in helping the kid adjust to their new environment.

Bowlby concludes that a kid develops an early mental image of the primary caregiver, or what he refers to as "internal working models," as stated in his book *Attachment and Loss*. This internal image of the primary caregiver serves as the child's model for developing relationships and setting expectations for how other people should behave.

As a child has their first interaction with another person, these internal representations are formed. This relationship creates a pattern of communication that can endure a lifetime and constitute the fundamental set of beliefs. The child builds comfort, security, affection, and expectations for how someone should treat them in this mental representation.

Critical Period for Developing an Attachment

According to Bowlby, there is a pivotal period for attachment development. The study of imprinting, where it is believed that young birds may only create a bond with their mother during a specific period shortly after hatching, is where the phrase is most frequently used. These factors have an impact on developmental processes like language acquisition, social bonding, and hearing and vision maturation.

Before neural connections become gradually more stable, important phases in the development of the nervous system are marked by significant levels of brain plasticity.

Brain connections become more secure as we age. Yet, the brain can get "stuck" and unable to adjust if it is overexposed to stress or loses a loved one at a young age. More challenges in maturity, such as anxiety and destructive conduct, may result from this. Relationships with attachment figures are essential for healthy development and play a crucial part in the development of one's neurobiological processes.

The development of spoken language skills, which are essential for the development of executive functions, is predicted by children's gestures, such as pride. Yet, the establishment of strong connections in the brain may prevent further modifications to its neuronal circuitry. For instance, the brain may not properly wire itself to process upcoming sensory inputs if a kid has atypical sensory experiences during this crucial period, such as auditory or visual deprivation.

Chapter 2:
The Attachment Styles

I n the 1970s, Mary Ainsworth carried out a significant study known as the *Strange Situation Study*. She examined how toddlers between the ages of 12 and 18 months reacted when their mother briefly left them alone.

The experiment started with the mother and child being placed in a room by themselves. Ainsworth observed the child to see if they were going to explore the room while their mother watched over them. Then a stranger would come in, talk to the mother, and go over to the child. After that, the mother would leave the room but quickly come back to comfort her child. Ainsworth developed the three main attachment styles—secure attachment, anxious attachment, and avoidant attachment—based on her observations of the children. According to the attachment theory, even though we might be unaware of it as adults, we preserve the memory of our relationship with our primary caregivers. As we get older, we look for companions that reflect that connection.

The strength of those ties is reflected in the attachment styles.

1. Because I feel comfortable letting individuals close to me depend on me, I am willing to depend on them.

2. I worry a lot that my partner does not truly care about me or would rather not be with me.

3. I have been in circumstances where people wanted me to have more intimate relationships than I am comfortable with.

The three styles are described in further detail below:

Secure Attachment Style

I find it simple to connect with other people. Since I feel comfortable having people depend on me, I am willing to depend on those close to me.

This attachment style, which is established by having a stable bond with one's primary caregiver, promotes healthy and long-lasting relationships. Parents or other caregivers do not need to be perfect for their children to have a secure attachment style.

Even if they mistake their child's nonverbal signals, these parents keep trying new approaches until their needs are met. The child can openly express their need for validation or reassurance because they are aware of their support and do not have to worry about being punished.

According to Ainsworth's study, children that had a secure attachment style exhibited the following behaviors:

- They felt comfortable enough to explore the room while their mother was present.
- When they felt frightened or uncertain, they looked to their mother for reassurance.
- They greeted their mother enthusiastically as she entered the room again.
- They chose to be with their mother over being with a stranger.

Early interactions with their primary caregiver help the child feel safe, understood, and valued. The primary caregiver is emotionally available to the child, which is why they feel this way. Furthermore, the person who is caring for them is conscious of their feelings and actions. The primary caregiver is the one whom the child learns from and imitates. You probably have a secure attachment style if any of the following apply to you:

- You can control your emotions.
- You can trust people.
- You have good communication skills.
- You can request emotional support.
- You feel at ease being alone.
- You feel at ease in close relationships.
- You are capable of introspection on your relationships.
- You can get along with people.
- You can resolve disagreements.
- You have high self-esteem.
- You can sustain emotional bonds in relationships.

Thus, those who maintain their secure attachment style throughout adulthood are emotionally stable and have healthy interpersonal communication skills. They give their partners trust, love, and emotional support.

Anxious Attachment Style

I am not happy with the degree of intimacy in my relationships. I often worry that the person I am with does not love or care about me or would rather not be with me.

When a child realizes they cannot rely on their primary caregiver to meet their needs, this attachment style develops. The causes of insecure attachment styles are inconsistent parenting and a lack of awareness of the child's needs. When the child is with their primary caregiver, they do not feel secure. Children who experience inconsistent parenting get confused.

Children with an anxious attachment style showed high discomfort in Ainsworth's experiment when the mother left the room.

Anxious attachment types are not only a result of inconsistent parenting. Traumatic experiences can also be a factor. Another factor is overly protective parents. In this situation, the child can sense their parents' concern and develop fear themselves.

Those who exhibit an anxious attachment style might have had a primary caregiver who:

- Comforted their child inconsistently. They may have coddled the child occasionally, but they may also have been uncaring or distant.
- Easily became overwhelmed.
- Swapped between paying the child attention and shooing them away.

- Made the child feel accountable for their feelings. It is thought that raising a child in this manner can make them codependent in the future. They learn early on that they are in charge of other people's emotions.

Indications that you may have an anxious attachment style include:

- Codependency
- Intense fears of rejection
- A reliance on your partner for emotional support or validation
- Clingy tendencies
- Hypersensitivity to criticism
- A need for external validation
- Jealousy issues
- Difficulty being alone
- Low self-esteem
- A sense of unworthiness of love
- Intense fear of abandonment
- Trust issues

The anxious attachment style can manifest in relationships as the following:

- The individual with this style does not feel deserving of love and needs constant validation from their partner.
- The person thinks that the problems in the relationship are their fault.
- The person's jealousy can be very extreme.

- The person may distrust their partner because of their poor self-esteem.
- The person may be highly sensitive to their partner's actions and emotions, making assumptions about their intentions.

These signs are all a result of a profound fear of abandonment. The person may desire an intimate relationship, but they are unable to build it because of their fear of being abandoned. People who have this attachment style might ignore their own needs in favor of attending to those of their partner.

Adults can also acquire characteristics of anxious attachment styles. Someone may exhibit elements of this style if they regularly deal with inconsistent behavior from their partner. The person may have anxiety or insecurity about the relationship if their partner is inconsistent in showing affection or is emotionally abusive. Abusive relationships are one illustration of this.

A person may come to believe it if they are in a relationship with a partner who consistently calls them stupid or incompetent. They might cling to their partner as a result of this belief. Because they do not believe they can manage on their own, they will rely on their partner to take care of them.

Avoidant Attachment Style

I find it difficult to get close to people and feel uncomfortable when people want to get close to me. I have been in situations where people wanted me to have more intimate relationships than I am comfortable with.

Fear of emotional and physical intimacy prevents people with an avoidant attachment style from developing long-term relationships. Children with primary caregivers who were harsh, emotionally distant, or unavailable have this attachment style. These people might have gone through the following as children:

- They were left to fend for themselves without support.
- They were required to act independently before they were ready.
- They were punished because they were dependent on their primary caregivers.
- When they voiced their feelings or needs, their primary caregivers rejected them.
- Their basic needs were not given a lot of attention.

While such primary caregivers may have acted in this manner as a result of blatant neglect, other people may have been overburdened with other duties. In either case, these kids developed into strong independent adults. They feel awkward turning to others for support or to meet their needs.

If any of the following describe you, you may have an avoidant attachment style:

- You avoid emotional or physical intimacy.
- You treat other people with contempt.
- You are unable to trust people.
- You become anxious when people try to get close to you.
- You stay away from social encounters.
- You think you can get along without other people.

- You struggle with commitment.

People with this attachment style maintain a distance in relationships. They never form relationships where emotional depth is experienced because they do not seek emotional intimacy.

The partners of those with avoidant attachment usually feel that they do not know them and are being stone-walled when the other person believes the relationship is growing too serious. Children with the avoidant attachment style in Ainsworth's experiment exhibited no preference between their mother and the stranger. They also did not turn to their mothers for comfort.

Chapter 3:
What Is Anxious Attachment?

An individual with anxious attachment has an unyielding pattern of behavior in which they constantly worry about being abandoned, depend on their relationships for emotional stability and comfort, and frequently look for reassurance. Anxious attachment causes insecurity when there is a separation, which in turn causes conflict with friends or family who might not want to continue supporting the person in this way.

Reaching out without feeling rejected by others might be challenging for someone who struggles with anxious attachment. For example, if someone has recently lost a loved one, they could find it difficult to talk about the loss or express their emotions out of concern that they will be judged as "weak" or "inadequate," even when what they need is acceptance and support. Because of this, anxious people typically wait until it is too late to get help.

A person with anxious attachment typically finds it difficult to make everyday decisions, such as going to school, relocating to a new place, or looking for a job. For instance, a person with anxious attachment may decide to put off starting a romantic relationship out of fear that they will be dumped by their partner.

The foundation of anxious attachment is the notion that human infants require an emotional bond with their caregiver to survive and thrive. If they are taken away from their primary caregivers, who are typically their parents, they frequently cry for hours and are not comforted until they are reunited with them. Some specialists contend that anxious attachment is a learned behavior, while others assert that it is a genetic trait that cannot be altered.

The development of the child's mind depends greatly on the need for this bond. The child will learn to trust others and feel secure in their relationships if the caregiver is regularly responsive and sensitive to their needs. Yet, if the caregiver is emotionally distant and/or unsupportive, the child is more likely to exhibit anxious behaviors when they face separation as adults.

When children first become conscious of their feelings in early childhood, anxious attachment patterns often emerge. These unfamiliar feelings start to terrify them, and they feel the need to seek out others' reassurance, especially their parents. To get the attention of their caregiver, they could cry, cling to them, or leap at loud noises. These behaviors serve as a defense mechanism to maintain strong emotional bonds with the caregiver even when they are briefly apart.

If a child realizes that manipulating others is the only way to gain acceptance and/or positive attention, anxious attachment becomes an issue. It can also become an issue if the child begins to feel that, to survive, they need to constantly be the center of attention or to hear that they are "special."

People with anxious attachment are frequently time-oriented, unrealistic about their goals, and unreasonable in their demands on others. They might, for instance, insist that their partner phone them every day after work, or they might ask someone else to decide on all of life's major choices, such as whom to marry and what career to pursue.

When people are worried about themselves, they also exhibit anxious attachment. Conversely, a person could feel unworthy in their professional or interpersonal relationships as a result of how they think others are reacting.

Typically, anxious attachment starts in childhood and shows up in romantic relationships as the child becomes older. Since they are terrified of being alone as adults, people with anxious attachment are frequently (but not always) in unhappy relationships. People may have relationship insecurity as a result of a loved one's death, a divorce, or even attending a wedding. To ensure that they are "good enough" to be their partner's romantic interest, these people may frequently check in with others via phone calls, texts, or in-person contact.

Those who struggle with anxious attachment frequently believe they have no control over their lives and struggle to make decisions without first seeking advice from others. For instance, people can decide to attend a gathering they do not want to go to because they worry about being alone. A person can even decide to attend college even though they do not want to because they are afraid of being alone.

Chapter 4:
Signs of Someone With Anxious Attachment

Signs of Anxious Attachment Style in Children

- They are unable to be consoled when distressed. When you try to comfort them, they will not react.
- They tend to attach to their caregivers.
- They are wary of new people.
- They struggle to build relationships with other children.
- There is a reluctance to explore their surroundings.
- They give off an agitated vibe all around.
- They have trouble managing or controlling their negative emotions.
- They behave aggressively.

Signs of Anxious Attachment Style in Adults

- They lack confidence and believe that others are better than them.
- They pay attention to their partner's needs while ignoring their own.
- They may harbor intense mistrust or resentment toward their relationship.
- They may become consumed with their relationship due to their fear of desertion.
- They do not like being by themselves.

- They have a low sense of self.
- They have an ongoing desire for intimacy and closeness.
- They have a fear of being abandoned.
- They excessively rely on their relationship.
- They continuously seek acceptance from others and are people-pleasers.
- They find it challenging to trust their partner. Because they were unable to rely on their caregiver as a child, they lack trust.
- They are extremely sensitive to their partner's emotions and behavior.
- They obsess over or overanalyze unimportant details.
- They have a pattern in which they do not feel love in their relationships.
- They over-attend to their partner's needs because they want them to be needed by them.
- They take on the majority of the blame and guilt in the relationship.

The following are examples of anxious attachment style behaviors:

- You keep texting or calling your partner until you hear back from them.
- You regularly visit their social media pages.
- When the relationship is peaceful, you feel suspicious.
- You take on extra projects at work to appease your coworkers, which causes you to overextend yourself.
- You inquire about your attractiveness to your lover regularly.

- Even when you are aware that a relationship is unhealthy for you, you will go to great lengths to keep it going.

People with anxious attachment style do not think they deserve love; they think they have to earn it from their partners. As we will see later, this dynamic typically results in an attraction between people with an anxious attachment style and people with an avoidant attachment style.

The anxious attached partner in such a relationship has to compete for the other's attention. They feel comfortable in this kind of relationship. On the other hand, they would find a partner who freely provides love and attention uninteresting.

Chapter 5:
Why Do We Fall Into Anxious Attachment?

R elationship anxiety is characterized by constant worry about one's partner, a need to appease them, a sense of inferiority toward others, and a propensity for jealousy or moodiness. Those who experience relationship anxiety frequently believe that their love is not appreciated or reciprocated.

People usually have anxious attachment when their parents were distant, unsupportive, or inconsistent in their upbringing. A child who is extremely insecure and has an anxious attachment to their primary caregiver is more likely to develop an anxious attachment in their marriage later.

Those who have relationship anxiety typically had a close friend or family member they could confide in when they were younger. This person or these people leaving caused that child to become quite apprehensive and concerned. This is because the young person felt as though their safety net had been compromised and lost.

Also, when a parent is overly protective of their child, anxious attachment might form. Because the parent appears to want the child just to be with them in this situation, the child may start to feel afraid.

Children who see or are exposed to abuse at home or whose parents are overly controlling may also experience anxious attachment.

If the parent is simply unavailable, anxious attachment might also develop. For instance, if a parent is depressed and unable to maintain their child, the youngster may get anxious and fear losing their support once more.

The rejection or severe punishment of a kid by a parent or other caregiver can also result in insecure attachment. This might occur if the child irritates the caregiver by being very outgoing, needy, or demanding. This child may start to experience anxiety and worry that their parent might not support them or love them.

Why Do We Get Stuck?

Those with an anxious attachment style may choose to stay in a relationship even though it is no longer what they want. They might think that no one else would value them enough to care for them or that no one else could provide for their needs. Also, they could worry excessively about what would happen if their partner leaves them or if they are rejected by others. The possibility exists because they value the other person highly. They may have been in a close relationship with this individual as children or they may have been their first love.

Those who experience relationship anxiety also worry excessively about what other people think of them. They fear being alone because they depend on the approval of others to feel secure. Because of this, it may be challenging for them to end a toxic relationship.

Why Do We End Up Hurting Ourselves?

Individuals who worry about relationships often, physically or emotionally, harm themselves as a result of their worries. They usually feel unlovable, unworthy, or rejected. Individuals who are worried about relationships constantly think negatively. They can believe that they are unfit to serve others or that if they reveal their true colors, people will not love them.

Those who experience this form of attachment are also more prone to mental problems like substance addiction, depression, and anxiety. Due to their fear of being rejected or of losing their partners, those who are worried about relationships may also experience extreme sadness.

They frequently do not feel understood when communicating since they are reluctant to express their hurt and pain.

Those who are anxious about relationships may find that their partners control their behavior. They prefer to carry out their partners' wishes.

Chapter 6:
How to Deal and Cope With Your Anxious Attachment Style ?

B uilding and maintaining healthy relationships may be challenging for someone with an anxious attachment style. Thankfully, there are steps you can do to manage your anxiety and develop solid relationships.

Before anything else, understand what an anxious attachment style is and how it affects your relationships.

According to Bowlby and Ainsworth, unstable relationships are a sign of anxious attachment. Individuals who exhibit this attachment style worry that their needs will not be met or that their partner may hurt them.

They consequently tend to be needy and clinging in relationships. They may struggle to settle down and stop fighting during an argument until their partner has met their need for reassurance.

Ultimately, this is an unhealthy behavior in relationships, and it is not something you should develop. It is crucial to understand that if you are dealing with this type of attachment, it can be addressed in therapy.

One of the most effective ways to resolve any issues that have arisen from your childhood is to speak with a mental health professional about your attachment style and how it affects your relationships. Receiving the assistance you require might have an impact on your present and future relationships as well as your life as a whole.

Overcoming Your Anxious Attachment Style

Working on your self-worth and self-esteem is one of the best strategies to get over an anxious attachment style. This can be achieved by keeping a journal, engaging in mindfulness exercises, or attending to any underlying problems that might be aggravating your anxiety.

When you start to feel better about yourself, it can be a sign that you are on the road to recovery and forming healthier relationships. Your relationships will get better as you begin to feel better about yourself.

Unresolved childhood traumas that had an impact on your sense of security, trust, and safety in relationships might cause anxious attachment. It is critical to recognize these experiences as soon as possible so that you can move past them and regain your ability to trust.

By concentrating on positive affirmations and learning to believe in yourself more, you can improve your self-esteem. It may take some time, but it is possible to get past anxious attachment.

Try to take a deep breath and relax if you are feeling anxious, depressed, or angry. To calm yourself down and distance yourself from the situation if you are feeling tense or anxious, try some yoga or meditation.

Another useful method for overcoming your anxious attachment style is to change the way you view the situation and think of your partner. You can gain confidence and begin to feel safer in your relationship if you can change the way you think about the situation and concentrate on your partner rather than playing the victim.

Finally, you can work on forgiving yourself and your previous relationships as well as practicing self-acceptance. It will be simpler to communicate honestly with others once you can understand your own emotions and forgive yourself. You will be able to do this to lead a life that is more rewarding overall and to have healthier relationships.

Key Indicators of Anxious Attachment

It is likely your partner has an anxious attachment style if you are in a relationship and are experiencing anxiety. This kind of relationship is built on insecurity and fear, which can result in a variety of destructive behaviors. Thankfully, there are approaches to dealing with and overcoming this style of attachment.

The type of ambivalent attachment known as anxious attachment is often the outcome of an unorganized bonding experience with caregivers during childhood. Trauma frequently causes this kind of relationship, which in turn causes several negative behaviors as an adult.

The major indications of this type of attachment include low self-esteem, increased anxiousness, and feeling of jealousy. You should seek therapy if your anxious attachment is preventing you from having a healthy relationship.

1. You are too clingy.

You can find yourself overly clinging to your partner if they have an anxious attachment to feel close and safe. This could make you feel trapped and alone in your relationship. You can believe that your partner is not giving you the attention or validation that you deserve, which is especially prevalent if they have poor self-esteem.

2. You need consistency.

One of the major indications of anxious attachment is that you often seek consistency in your relationship with your partner. You can falsely assume that your partner no longer loves you or that you are not compatible with them if they start acting differently.

3. You overthink everything.

You tend to imagine the worst-case scenario too quickly when you have an anxious attachment. This can result in anxiety, which might set off your fight-or-flight response and impair your ability to think rationally.

4. You are angry when someone does not call you back.

When someone does not reach out to you, anxiety might make you angry and frustrated. If you have been dealing with anxiety for a while, this can be extremely stressful.

5. You are angry when people do not smile at you.

When others fail to appreciate you or show you affection, you may develop an anxious attachment. This can be challenging to deal with because you probably want your partner to see your efforts and appreciate them more.

6. Your partner is not compassionate about you.

It can be challenging to maintain a healthy and happy relationship with your partner if they are not supportive of you. This is especially true if your partner exhibits an anxious attachment style because they will not be able to tell you they do not care about you without making you feel uncomfortable. They might also criticize you, which would make you feel even more anxious.

Finding out more about your attachment style and making an effort to alter it are the best ways to approach this. Although it can be difficult at times, this process is ultimately beneficial.

If you are an adult with an anxious attachment style, it is important to work on your anxiety and insecurities so that you can have healthier relationships with your partner. The most effective way to do this is by working with a therapist to improve your communication skills and to learn healthy ways to set and keep boundaries.

Another approach for controlling your anxious attachment is to practice mindful breathing. You can concentrate better on what is going on around you if you breathe in and out through your nose.

What Can You Do to Help a Friend With Anxious Attachment?

The first step in helping a person with anxious attachment is to make them feel safe and secure. This can be done through consistent boundaries, managing and reinforcing rules and expectations, and showing them that their feelings can be managed.

Another way to help someone with anxious attachment is to provide them with positive reinforcement, which can reduce their stress levels. They can also learn to identify their triggers and work to avoid them. Those are anything that can trigger a person's anxiety and have an automatic reaction to them. Some examples of triggers are when a loved one is not present or focuses on other things, or when someone tries to pull away from them.

A person with an anxious attachment needs reassurance and constant love to feel safe, so when they are with someone emotionally unavailable or dismissive it can trigger their anxiety. They need to feel like they are being valued and worth it in their relationships. They can also have issues with trusting others. This can lead to feeling unsure of their ability to form a healthy relationship.

When an anxious attachment person meets new people, it can cause them to get very anxious and overwhelmed. The reason why they are anxious is that they do not know who the new person is, and it can be difficult to control their emotions in this situation.

Anxiety can also be triggered when a person is in the spotlight or when they are interacting with lots of people. This can cause the person to have more opinions and a greater need to please others, which can increase their anxiety even further.

If a person with an anxious attachment is dating, it can be extremely difficult to meet their needs. It can take a lot of self-work and awareness to create a more secure connection with a partner, but it can be done.

Therapists can help a person with anxious attachment break negative patterns and develop healthier behaviors in relationships. Taking the time to address past trauma and attachment wounds can help individuals turn their anxious attachment style into secure attachment so that they can be more fulfilled in their relationships.

The best thing you can do for a person with an anxious attachment is to talk about these issues with them. Having an open conversation about these issues can help them feel more connected to themselves and understand how their childhood experiences have affected them today.

Chapter 7:
Signs of an Anxious Attachment in a Relationship

O ne of life's best parts could be a relationship, especially one that is healthy and happy. But sadly, relationships are not always like this.

There are instances when problems develop in a relationship because of anxiety on the part of one or both partners, or anxieties brought on by external factors like work.

It is critical to recognize the symptoms of an anxious attachment in a relationship for both those who experience anxiety as well as those who care for someone who does.

The following is a list of indicators of a relationship with a highly anxious form of attachment:

1. Always trying to be overly nice and accommodating

When one or both partners always strive to be accommodating and appealing, it may be a sign that there is an anxious attachment present. This is a harmful way for people to interact with one another. Due to the ongoing need to please one another, neither partner feels as though they are receiving the time and attention they deserve, which can produce resentment and a lack of connection.

2. Difficulty setting and communicating boundaries

The inability to communicate and establish clear boundaries is another indication of an anxious attachment. To hold back their own needs, partners may frequently "go out of their way" to try to please one another. When both partners' needs continue to be unfulfilled, this kind of relationship can also result in a great deal of animosity in the future.

3. Scarcity mentality

A scarcity mentality can indicate that one or both couples have an anxious attachment. The scarcity mentality is the conviction that everything in the world is against us, whether it be work, money, love, or anything else. It may result from having unrealistic expectations and anxiety about the future, as well as being a trait of many unemployed people who lack negotiating and money management skills.

4. Difficulty staying faithful

Partners frequently become less happy and more irritable when they get jealous and possessive. Another unhealthy way of relating is that they could struggle to remain loyal.

5. Tendency to break up

When someone tends to end their relationship with their partner after a while, it may be an indication of an anxious attachment. They often believe that if they remain in a relationship "for the long haul," their partner would stop loving them; hence, they leave the relationship on their own terms before they get hurt. Both partners may feel a great deal of guilt as a result, and the one who was hurt may also feel resentment.

6. Unreasonable expectations

When someone has unreasonably high expectations for their relationships, that is another red flag of an anxious attachment. For instance, one partner might anticipate that the other will always fulfill all of their needs, every day. This kind of unrealistic expectation can cause a great deal of bitterness and weaken the feeling of love and connection.

7. Lack of appreciation

When one or both partners do not appreciate all that the other does for them, that is another indication that there may be an anxious attachment in the relationship. They might also find it hard to comprehend how difficult it is for people with anxiety to get over those challenges daily.

8. An inability to accept help

Not being able to accept assistance from a partner is unquestionably a hallmark of an anxious attachment. Partners may persistently insist that they are not deserving of or in need of assistance.

9. An inability to talk about problems

For fear of rejection or judgment, partners who have an anxious attachment style may find it challenging to discuss their issues with one another. They can avoid communication because they fear offending their partner.

10. Difficulty confronting their fears

Anxious attachment style partners could find it difficult to discuss their concerns and anxieties with one another. Over time, this could cause a great deal of angst, bitterness, and alienation in the relationship.

Chapter 8:
The Effects of Anxious Attachment on Romantic Relationships

According to the attachment theory, the relationships we aspire to have as adults are influenced by the relationships we had as children. Secure, anxious, and avoidant attachment styles are the three main types. You can decide if a certain love relationship is good for you by knowing your attachment style.

Secure attachers provide solid relationships based on trust and a sense of security. Knowing that their attachment figure will be there for them in times of need gives them a sense of security. They strive to form meaningful relationships and have a high level of empathy for others.

Conversely, anxious attachers often find it difficult to feel comfortable in their love lives. They do every effort to prevent rejection and desertion since they have a tremendous fear of both. To keep their partner away from their negativity and to keep them from leaving, they could become very guarded and avoid contact with them.

This can be especially risky in a committed, close-knit relationship. Conflicts, tensions, and disagreements may also result from it.

Fortunately, there are several strategies that people with anxious attachment can use to improve their relationships. Finding encouraging role models and adopting their actions can be a good place to start.

They can also try counseling to address the underlying causes of their anxiety and discover better methods to interact with people.

Anxious attachment jealousy is among the most common issues that persons with anxious attachment face in a romantic relationship. In essence, this is the feeling that a person with an anxious attachment will have that their partner will be more desirable than they are.

Anxious attachers put a lot of effort into their relationships and work hard to ensure they receive the attention they need. Also, they frequently worry about their partners' feelings and watch out for any indications that they might be growing distant from them.

A partner with an anxious attachment may start to behave in ways that show anger or insecurity when they are unhappy or feeling unappreciated. They might start to engage in harmful behavior, such as yelling or cutting.

It can be challenging for an anxious attacher to communicate their feelings to their partner, but by discussing their concerns and fears with them, you might be able to assist them in doing so. To assist them in identifying the spots in their bodies where they store their emotions, try body mapping or body scan meditation.

By demonstrating their importance to you and keeping open lines of communication, your partner may also be able to assist you in managing your anxious attachment. They might also be open to discussing their anxiety and any associated issues in your relationship with a therapist.

The traits of an anxious attachment style can be difficult to manage on your own, but they can be altered. By figuring out how to identify your anxious attachment patterns and then finding out how to deal with them in a way that makes you feel safe and loved, you can improve your relationship. It will take some time and consistency though.

Is Anxious Attachment Toxic in Relationships?

Anxious attachment is a type of insecure attachment that can be toxic in relationships. It can produce intense feelings of anxiety, self-doubt, and unhappiness. This may result in unhealthy behaviors, such as being overly jealous and controlling.

How to Manage Anxious Attachment in Relationships?

The most important thing to keep in mind when dealing with an anxiously attached partner is that their behavior can be an involuntary response to something you have not done. It is a normal part of their emotional process, and you should learn how to change the way you react to them to stop them from controlling you.

Triggers for Anxious Attachment

Being set off by their partner's actions or words is one of the most common triggers for someone who is anxiously attached. This may occur if they believe their partner does not value them, treats them disrespectfully, or ignores them.

An anxiously attached person's dread of being excluded or rejected may be the cause of this. Those who struggle with anxiety frequently experience excessive emotion, and some even cry out in frustration. This is because anxiety may make it very difficult to control your emotions.

Although it might be challenging to overcome insecure attachment, which is a reaction to past experiences, it is possible to learn how to do so and try to establish more safe, healthy ties in your life. Consider working with a therapist to pinpoint your triggers and develop healthy coping mechanisms if you have anxious attachment.

How to Overcome Anxious Attachment in Dating?

Being in a relationship with someone who has an anxious attachment style can be challenging because of how intense and demanding they can be. It could be difficult for them to maintain a new relationship over time since they become fixated on it and want to commit right away.

Try to set clear, consistent boundaries for them to follow to prevent this. Also, you can provide positive reinforcement by praising them for a job well done or their good behavior.

Furthermore, it is critical to constantly speak with your partner and let them know how much they mean to you. They may feel safer in the relationship and be more sympathetic toward you if you let them know how important they are to you.

How to Date With Anxious Attachment?

Dating and relationships might be challenging if you have an anxious attachment style. This attachment style is a result of trauma experienced as a child, but there are ways to deal with them and achieve happy romantic relationships.

To create a more comfortable connection with yourself, start by becoming conscious of your anxious attachment style. Make a conscious effort to date a secure person who can satisfy your emotional needs. According to relationship expert Sarah Lippman-Barile, doing this can aid in overcoming your emotions of anxiety and fostering a more secure relationship with your partner.

Be conscious of your anxiety and let the person you are dating know about it explicitly so they can help you face your fears. Knowing your attachment style might be a crucial first step since it will help you handle your partner more effectively when they exhibit signs of an anxious attachment style. Dates that just make you more anxious should be avoided. This can involve dating narcissists or avoidant people who cannot take care of your emotional needs. It is crucial to remember that everyone has a mix of baggage and problems to deal with.

If you tend to become worried easily, you might want to keep the first few dates lighthearted and enjoyable as you get to know each other better.

Next, work your way up to more intimate dates where you can both openly discuss your innermost concerns and secrets. You can use these early dates to establish trust while also figuring out whether or not you click with your partner. Speaking with a counselor or therapist can help you figure out what is going on and work through it together when you are unsure.

Can Anxious Attachment People Date Each Other?

It might be challenging to know how to proceed in a relationship with someone who has an anxious attachment style. You can be concerned about whether or not you can satisfy their needs or if they will feel comfortable in your presence. Do not allow your anxieties to stop you from dating though.

If you are honest about your needs, you can still date someone who has an anxious attachment style. It is crucial to communicate your needs to your partner to maintain a strong and fulfilling relationship.

For a relationship to be successful, communication is essential. If you have an anxious attachment style, this is even more important. It is common for people with this sort of attachment to have problems expressing their needs and wants to others because they may feel too anxious or overwhelmed to speak up.

This can be especially upsetting if you are in a relationship and discover that your partner is not providing for your needs in the way you would like. Talking through your feelings with a therapist can be beneficial if you are struggling with this.

Therapy can help you to better understand your anxiety and discover healthier coping mechanisms. Knowing your attachment style and how it affects your relationships can also be helpful.

Identifying your attachment style can help you avoid wasting time on dates with someone who will not fulfill your needs, which is another great way to improve your dating life. A therapist will be able to help you through this process and provide you with some advice on how to approach the dating world more effectively.

Early in their relationships, before they have a chance to seriously evaluate compatibility or measure how the other person would treat them, anxious attachers date a lot. Whilst it might be a tiring and stressful moment, it is vital to realize that this stage is common for anxious attachment people.

In the end, it is best to stick with a few love interests and figure out what works for you. You will have a better idea of how your relationship will progress and it will be much simpler to determine when it is time to part ways.

To learn how to express your needs and feelings to your partner more clearly, you can work with a therapist. It is less likely to waste time on relationships that do not work for your anxious attachment style. If you are prepared to put in the time and effort to take care of your partner's emotional needs as well as your own, your relationship can be incredibly fulfilling. The ideal partner will understand your attachment style and be able to assist you with it.

The secret to a successful relationship is managing your anxiety, and you can do this by making sure your partner is a decent person who respects you.

How to Date Someone With an Anxious Attachment Style?

You probably already know that people who have an anxious attachment style have a lot of emotions. It can be advantageous, but if you do not know how to handle their emotions, it can also result in some major issues.

Because of this, it is crucial to know your partner's attachment style before you start dating them. This will enable you to make a more informed decision about the best match for you.

You should always give your partner the reassurance they need to express their feelings. To let them know that you are thinking of them and that you want them to be in your life, all it takes is a quick text or phone call.

People with anxious attachment styles often have many fears and anxieties about the future, thus reassurance is crucial for them. It is a great way to keep them around for the long run because they frequently need to know that you will stand up for them if they ever feel threatened.

Being a good listener is another essential component of reassuring someone. Giving your partner a forum for the expression of their emotions can be therapeutic for them. If you are a good listener and demonstrate your concern for them, it may also be highly advantageous for your relationship.

Being a good listener to anxious partners can be very challenging since they require so much affirmation and reassurance. Although having to reassure them so constantly can be taxing, doing so will increase the likelihood that they will commit to the relationship over time.

Giving them some time to absorb their emotions and discuss their problems with you is a smart idea as well. Your partner may go through a significant healing process and grow more optimistic about their future with you as a result.

You can utilize the reassurance you give to encourage your partner to confide in you about their fears and anxieties, which will help you forge a strong emotional bond that will last the test of time.

If you have an anxious attachment style yourself, you can also try to avoid dating someone who does, as this will just make your fears and fear of being alone worse. You will be able to let go of your fears and anxieties and learn how to live with them securely and healthily if you have a secure attachment style.

It is not impossible to date someone who has an anxious attachment style, but before you commit to any form of relationship, you should do some research to determine if they are the appropriate fit for you. When you are first starting to date, it can be a scary undertaking, but it is worth it!

What Is the Hardest Attachment Style to Date?

A person's attachment style forms in early childhood based on their relationships with their earliest caregivers. Those who grew up with trustworthy caregivers who consistently engaged in loving, nurturing ways tend to have healthy attachment styles and develop strong connections as adults.

The most common attachment style is secure, where the individual feels comfortable and secure with a partner and has healthy, stable relationships. People who grew up with insecure caregivers or unhealthy relationships tend to have an anxious or avoidant attachment style, depending on how their childhood experiences shaped them.

Many factors influence the development of your attachment style, but they are most often affected by your relationship with your earliest caregivers. These caregivers have a profound impact on your feelings of trust, safety, and security.

Those with an anxious attachment style, for example, will feel as though they do not know whether or not their needs are being met. They also may become frightened and irritable, which makes it hard for them to form healthy relationships.

On the other hand, those with an avoidant attachment style will often feel as though they do not have a clear idea of their partner's feelings or how much they love them. This can cause them to rely on their sense of self-worth and independence, which can lead them to feel more threatened by the possibility of getting close to a potential partner.

Some research has found that the two least compatible personality types are those who are anxious and avoidant, a phenomenon known as "split personalities." This is largely a result of how our earliest caregivers influenced our attachment styles.

If you are in a relationship with someone who has an anxious attachment style, you might try to make them feel safe and protected. They will likely react to your actions or behaviors in a way that is reminiscent of what they felt as children, so it can be helpful to give them consistent feedback, pay attention to their emotions, and communicate openly with them.

Anxiously attached individuals may be extremely clingy and possessive, especially if they have experienced some kind of trauma. They can also have low self-esteem and a poor relationship with their bodies, which can make them feel as though they are not enough for a partner.

While these types of attachment styles can be hard to change, there are ways to overcome them. In the most difficult cases, a trained mental health professional can help you work through your fears and anxieties.

One of the hardest attachment styles to date is disorganized attachment, a rare type that combines the traits of anxiety and avoidance. These individuals crave a sense of connection, but they're anxious about letting someone in, says Marni Feuerman, PsyD, LCSW, a psychotherapist in private practice.

The most challenging part about dealing with someone who has this attachment style is the fact that you will have to figure out how to navigate their confusing behavior and mixed signals. The best thing to do is to reassure them that you are there for them and that you care about their well-being. This can be a lot easier said than done, but it is worth trying.

Chapter 9:
Cultivate the Relationship You Have and Strengthen the Feeling of Security

C ultivating relationships entails fostering feelings of security and attachment by emphasizing pleasant interactions and establishing trust. It also means fostering a sense of autonomy by learning how to deal with daily challenges that could otherwise result in relationship strain or dissolution.

Many people's lives are heavily centered around their relationships. They provide us with a sense of belonging by allowing us to feel loved and connected. In relationships, we want the other person to desire and love us as much as we do them. Because we are dependent on this other person to survive, we are quite bonded to them. We all yearn for affection and love. As a result, when we think that this other person might leave us, we become anxious. The more attachment we develop to this individual, the worse it will hurt if we have to part ways or get rejected. Our relationship may suffer as a result of this persistent and severe anxiety and sadness, especially if it lasts for an extended period.

Relationships are about supporting, embracing, and understanding one another. The mutual attachment and feeling of security are what matter. We can feel confident when we have a strong connection with someone because we know they will support us in the event of a crisis. But, if they begin to ignore us or reject us, it can be extremely worrying because, in our minds, it suggests that they could abandon us at any time. It might even be replaced by excitement about finding out what happens next.

You can learn how to cultivate relationships and boost the feeling of security by following these simple steps:

1. Relax your body and mind.

To relax your body and mind, you need to stop worrying about the other person. Prioritize your well-being. Spend some time considering whether you are sleeping enough, eating healthily, and getting the right amount of exercise.

Recognize your physical self, but avoid becoming fixated on it. Spend a few minutes before going to sleep taking long, deep breaths. As you take deep breaths in and out, chant a peaceful mantra while listening to relaxing music. Choose a calming, introspective activity that you enjoy. Try keeping a journal or playing your preferred music.

2. Understand that intimacy can help you cope.

The hardest step is always this one. We have frequently experienced rejection or hurt by loved ones. It is crucial to be able to deal with these feelings of loneliness and detachment since they can leave us feeling incredibly sad and terrified.

Intimacy is a two-way process. It functions best when both partners are at ease and confident enough to open up to one another about their inner thoughts and feelings. Intimacy strengthens the bonds between members of a family or a relationship. Personal intimacy is another option, which entails getting closer to yourself every day.

3. Accept that fears are a natural part of being close to someone.

We all have worries, and as we age and encounter more painful situations or serious illnesses, our fears grow.

Our memories of the past are usually the source of our fears. Although overcoming these fears might be challenging, it is an essential step in learning how to trust others after being injured in the past.

4. Gain self-worth and confidence.

It takes effort to develop the skills needed to build secure and strong relationships. You do not have to do it alone, though. Making new acquaintances, enhancing your skills, and increasing your involvement in volunteer work are all ways to boost your confidence and sense of worth.

Feeling that you matter to other people and that your life matters is a key component of self-worth. Doing things for yourself and others should be your first step. Volunteer at a hospital or school.

5. Allow yourself to see the other person as a friend.

This is a crucial phase because it allows you to go past your fears, worries, anger, resentment, and desire for revenge and instead see what is possible in the relationship. Keep the relationship from taking precedence over your self-worth.

Let yourself see the other person as a friend who is doing their best to assist you, rather than as a threat or an opponent. Recognize that just because someone makes mistakes does not mean they are trying to hurt you.

You reduce your fear of being rejected by developing the relationship and strengthening your feeling of security. We can confront our anxiety and comprehend why we feel so worried by doing this. If we calmly approach them, we can also see that they do not want to offend us and will not reject or leave us as a result.

We can start reducing our feelings of anxiety and insecurity by understanding what causes them. The most effective approach might be to forge closer ties with those who might desert us or otherwise reject us. This entails increasing the feeling of security and cultivating the relationship by carrying out normal things.

In general, it might be challenging for you to accept someone's actions when you feel hurt by them, especially if they are close to you. However, keep in mind that experiencing pain or rejection is a crucial stage in our development. It teaches us how to deal with difficulties in life and prevents us from becoming overly reliant on other people. It is not simple, but if we can face our fears and accept that we do not need to control our relationships, we can become more intimate with the people who matter to us.

Chapter 10:
The Ultimate Dating Exercises

The Dating Dilemma

When you have an anxious attachment style, dating can be challenging, and you might worry that you will never find the right partner. First dates could go smoothly at the beginning but quickly spiral as repressed anxieties start to surface. You can find yourself stressing excessively over getting a second date and, as a result, failing to pay attention to your date. When you are worried about what might happen, you can be afraid even to start dating. As a result, many people who have an anxious attachment style stop being present on dates because they find it difficult to let go of all their worries that something might go wrong.

Daily Exercises

You can use some daily activities to reduce your dating anxiety. If you want to be in or are already in a more serious relationship, these exercises can help you. They can also help you if you are casually dating. Whatever stage you are at, developing a more honest relationship with yourself and your emotions will help you learn to overcome your anxiety and build stronger relationships. Since human beings require closeness to thrive, denying yourself of it can only cause you harm and deprive you of many of life's pleasures.

Spend time engaging in physical intimacy. Each day, you should strive for cuddling, hugging, kissing, or any other physical activity that makes you feel more intimate with your partner. You do not have to be sexual, though it is certainly a choice you can make. You can spend some time hugging friends or other loved ones if you do not currently have a significant other so that you can feel some kind of physical closeness. When you can establish that physical bond, your anxiety will start to lessen, and you will develop the habit of being more open with your body and enabling other people to approach you physically. People are more likely to get emotionally close after you allow for physical intimacy.

Learn to let your date or partner speak uninterrupted for ten minutes, and ask them to do the same for you. While this is not the ideal way to communicate all the time, you can try this exercise once daily to help everyone become better listeners. Everyone does not feel as though others are talking over them when each person has their own designated time to speak, and you learn to hold off on responding until you have thoroughly listened to your partner. When you do not listen carefully, you could make snap judgments and react out of fear before you completely comprehend how complex the situation is. When someone does not get the opportunity to express their opinions, they may start to feel insecure and can blow minor issues out of proportion.

Have a daily conversation about each person's needs and how they felt the other has not met them. It only needs five minutes or so, but you should feel at ease enough to handle any problems before they get out of hand. You do not have to do this every day if your relationship is casual or young, but you should express your feelings anytime a problem arises. In other relationships, you should also try to have these candid discussions; doing so can be great practice. Even though not everyone responds favorably to these conversations, you must make an effort to facilitate them if you want to build strong bonds that do not turn clingy or passive-aggressive.

Spend some time enjoying one another's hobbies. In a partnership, you work as a team with the other person, and even if they have interests that you do not share, you still need to respect their interests. They will begin to feel ashamed if you ignore what they enjoy, which will cause anxiety. You should expect that your partner will respect your interests just as much as you do. Try to engage in that interest to some extent; at the absolute least, ask about it and allow them to share their thoughts.

Set objectives in your relationships. Both of you should set goals for the relationship, and you can check in daily to see how they are going. These objectives are useful because they enable you to identify your needs and desires. Goals ensure that you take the journey together, so no one feels like they are left behind in the relationship or that they have to sacrifice a lot.

Mindfulness Exercises

One of the most important qualities you can have in a relationship is mindfulness because it enables you to be present in the now without allowing worries about the future or the past to pull you away from what is occurring right now. As you interact with new or long-term relationships, pay attention to how you feel. To help you stay present, use all of your senses. What does the room look like? How is the other person's facial expression? How do you feel? What flavor can you currently taste? You remain in the present moment when you tune into your senses. After dates, this mindfulness should remain. Give yourself some time to reflect. Have you had any fun? What caused you to feel very uncomfortable or unhappy? What potential do you see for that relationship? Sometimes dates do not go well, so do not let rejection negatively affect your future relationships. Instead, take rejection in stride. Instead of getting sucked into your troubled past relationships, remind yourself that you have the present to improve. When you approach dating mindfully, you make opportunities for development and introspection and prevent yourself from allowing negative experiences to hold you back.

Vulnerability Exercises

For persons with anxious attachment styles, vulnerability is difficult. The capacity to be open and honest about our feelings, fears and needs is known as vulnerability. In the end, our vulnerability makes it possible for us to connect with others. Brene Brown, a renowned psychologist, identified the importance of vulnerability in relationships. According to her, people today tend to suffer from intimacy because they find it difficult to be vulnerable with other people in their lives. But without that intimacy, it can be challenging to keep a love relationship going. To promote trust, communication, and relationship growth, you must be vulnerable.

When you need something, ask for it. Your date or partner is not obligated to give you what you want, and you should not pressure them to do so if they are not ready, able, or willing to do so. If you feel that your partner is not being vulnerable with you, try starting the conversation by sharing a bit of yourself. If that does not work, you can also say that you would like to know them better. You can inform a person that they need to be more cautious when discussing an issue if they do something that triggers you. Again, you cannot compel someone to change, but in a relationship, partners should be understanding of one another's emotional and physical needs. The problem is that a lot of people do not express their needs, thus the other person is unaware that they are there. If you do not ask, the answer "yes" is not an option!

Although vulnerability takes time to develop, you can speed it up by expressing yourself honestly. Do not just say you are fine when your partner asks if you are angry, to keep the peace. Shaking the Coke bottle to make it burst when you finally open it is all you are doing, not keeping the peace. While cracking the cap open on an undisturbed Coke bottle will generate a little hiss, it will only result in a minor hiccup. The best course of action is to express your anger immediately since, if you do not, the negative thought patterns have time to set in and you can start to ruminate, which heightens your anxiety. Even though it may not be enjoyable, expressing your negative feelings might help you calmly resolve problems.

When you feel the need to lie to your partner or avoid discussing a subject with them, ask yourself why you feel that way. If there were not a deeper reason, you would not feel the need to keep that information a secret from your partner. Hence, there must be one. You tend to hide the things that make you feel ashamed, but keep in mind that shame is an inappropriate emotion that ignores the complexity of humanity. When you can share with your partner the thing that makes you feel the worst about yourself, you are revealing the most vulnerable aspects of yourself. Furthermore, once you reveal those aspects of yourself, you start to believe that "They will love me no matter what just because I am me, and they can love my flaws, even when I struggle to love them myself." Although it hurts, admitting you are mistaken can strengthen relationships.

When you are vulnerable, you can remain true to yourself. You do not simply run away from problems. You confront the problems head-on and let your partner see all sides of you, including the challenging ones. You express your emotions and stop letting fear and shame control your interactions with others. Whether you like it or not, sharing challenges is a necessary part of being vulnerable. To let the light in—the hope, the togetherness, and the love—you must thus open the darkest portions of yourself in whatever manner you can.

Trust-Building Exercises

When one or both partners in a relationship exhibit anxious attachment styles, trust-building is especially crucial because the anxiety can make a person fearful of possible abandonment and that their partner will cheat on them or engage in other behaviors that would undermine the trust in the relationship. Since trust must be established on both sides, these activities are beneficial for both the anxious attachment sufferer and their partner.

Maintain healthy boundaries. Even though you may be tempted to check on what they are doing, give your partner the space they need. Reduce the frequency of your relationship check-ins as a challenge to yourself.

Tell your partner something about you that they do not know, and ask them to tell you something about themselves that you do not know. No matter how well you think you know someone, there is always more to discover, so make time to check in with one another and strengthen your bond.

Exercises that build trust between you and your partner can benefit both of you. Even though it may seem foolish, practicing trust falls or guiding your partner through an obstacle course while they are blindfolded can help you and your partner reestablish a missing trust connection. Moreover, you might want to give different exercises, like couple's yoga, a try.

Communication Exercises

One of the most important aspects of every relationship is communication because, without it, you lack the resources you need to foster openness and trust. Conversation guarantees that you talk things out before you react badly and enables you to respond to your issues in different ways. All partners should try to complete these exercises regularly for the best benefits. These exercises will assist all attachment styles, especially the insecure one. It is time to start talking, but also to start communicating in a variety of other ways.

Whenever you experience anxiety, let your partner know, and encourage them to share their feelings as well. You must create an open channel of communication for when someone is concerned about the health of the relationship, just as you did when you first became more vulnerable. You are not required to keep your activities to speaking alone. You can, for instance, express yourself in writing. How you are feeling can be expressed in a shared notebook, and doing so can facilitate a conversation free of conflict. You must be careful when writing to avoid being passive-aggressive.

There is much more to communication than just speaking or writing. As a result, you must develop your listening skills; you cannot simply listen at a basic level. Learn to listen actively. Active listening entails paying close attention to what is being said by others while avoiding interruptions. You do not try to reprimand them or tell them how to feel; you just let them speak. Instead, you spend time listening to them as they describe how they are feeling and how they see the world. After they have finished speaking, you can ask them follow-up questions to elicit more information and foster empathy rather than to express your feelings. "I suppose what you are trying to say here is ..." is a good way to express how you think they are feeling. Likewise, be honest about what you do not understand by expressing something like, "I am not sure I understand that part of what you said. Could you just rephrase that?" Once you have as fully as possible comprehended the other person's point of view, you will eventually get the chance to speak; nevertheless, as you listen, do not try to prepare your responses in advance. Before you formulate your reaction and communicate your feelings, fully comprehend the other person's true point of view. Because it makes both parties feel heard, this type of mutual listening will allay any concerns.

You and your partner need to work harder at expressing thanks to one another. Every day, look for something to be thankful for in your relationship. If you are casually dating, try to find something positive about the experience. Even if a date does not go as planned, you can still be thankful for the lessons you learned from it or how it helped you find future dates that did. Gratitude should be communicative because when you appreciate someone, you should tell them that you appreciate them! While it is common knowledge that dates are aware of their preferences for particular traits or behaviors, other people cannot read your mind and may not even be adept at interpreting your body language. Even if it sounds cliché, everyone likes to be complimented since verbal affirmations make people feel better than being left to assume. Do not show gratitude merely out of obligation; however, do so. Then, because you both deserve recognition, your partner should do the same for you.

Try to spend time each week communicating without being interrupted by a phone. While you are on a date, you do not need to constantly have your phone in your hand or check your work email. Even if it only lasts for a moment, the other person feels the disconnect. Individuals desire a love relationship that makes them feel engaged. You would not want someone else to be glued to their phone. That disconnect would promote anxiety while limiting vulnerable communication because no one wants to be vulnerable when they sense the other person is only half-listening.

When you begin to communicate, you and your partner will have less to worry about. You will become a better date, and you will learn to have deeper, more vulnerable relationships that will leave you feeling self-assured rather than filled with shame.

Chapter 11:
The Effects of Anxious Attachment on Professional Relationships

How a person interacts with others at work is crucial in a society where social interaction can be essential to career success. This is particularly true when a person's attachment style significantly affects their interpersonal interactions, and it might be important to understand how different attachment styles affect outcomes at work.

Anxiety and avoidance are traits of an insecure attachment style, which has a significant impact on how you feel at work. This kind of person typically has low self-esteem and is easily upset or depressed.

They often require reassurance that everything is well from their partners or other individuals. They might find it difficult to trust their supervisors or coworkers, and they might be more likely to react angrily. They can easily become overwhelmed and struggle to cope with change or challenges.

These are the same qualities that hinder them from being good team leaders or managers at work. Employees with an insecure attachment style are more likely to struggle with communication, getting along with coworkers, and making decisions when working in a team.

Your ability to get employment may be hampered by an insecure attachment style, which can also lower your level of career satisfaction. There are, nonetheless, things you may do to enhance your circumstance and raise your possibilities of locating a rewarding profession. To convince your supervisor and coworkers to respect your boundaries and support your success in the workplace, for instance, you may be more forthcoming and communicative with them.

Anxious Attachment at Work

Anxious attachment sufferers frequently overanalyze and overthink things and feel insecure. They are continuously looking for acceptance and worry about losing relationships. They may struggle to accept constructive criticism because they fear receiving negative feedback.

Anxious employees may find it more difficult to function independently because they may cling to their managers and bosses to gain their acceptance and approval. Also, they are more prone than secure employees to become burned out and want to quit their jobs soon.

This can have disastrous effects on the business sector, especially for small enterprises. It can imply that a nearby company must shut down or relocate.

A bankruptcy may also adversely influence the credit ratings of further businesses that might think about setting up shops in the municipality, which may have an immediate effect on their profitability and growth.

However, due to how this would affect the nearby communities, it may also have a direct effect on the economy as a whole. As a result, some companies may decide to relocate to a different area that is unaffected by bankruptcy.

The Effects of Anxious Attachment on Professional Relationships

Individuals with this attachment type may be clingy and needy toward their peers and leaders, which has a major impact on their ability to maintain professional relationships. Also, they are more prone to believe that their superiors and coworkers do not appreciate them, which could eventually result in a decline in their well-being. They might be prone to getting annoyed or angry with people, which might make them seem unprofessional. They may also be distant and reclusive toward others, which can hinder learning and innovation.

The effects of an anxious attachment style at work are a complicated matter that calls for thorough consideration and patience. These problems can be addressed and overcome, though. Realizing that there is a problem requires the first step of seeking help from a dependable coach, friend, or therapist. You can start creating solutions for enhancing your emotional and interpersonal functioning at work after you can talk through the problem.

Career Connections: Understanding Your Attachment Style

By enabling you to form secure, reliable, and trusting relationships, your attachment style can assist you in making decisions about your professional and personal relationships. Also, it might aid in maintaining your self-esteem and building a positive reputation.

If you become more involved in the community or assume leadership responsibilities, you can leverage your attachment style to your advantage. You may be able to control your stress levels and make wiser judgments at work with its assistance.

Understanding your attachment style can also be a useful tool for helping you in dealing with difficulties at work, such as working with a new supervisor. It can assist you in realizing that you may feel more confident with your coworkers than with other corporate executives, and it can also enable you to take action to improve your interactions.

Counselors can also benefit from being aware of how your attachment style can impact how well you get along with coworkers. With the use of this knowledge, you may better comprehend the expectations and needs of your clients and direct them toward a productive working relationship.

This is especially true for those who have been unemployed for an extended period or are unable to find fulfillment in their current position. They can be required to adopt a different strategy or set distinct objectives from other employees.

For instance, if you have a secure attachment, you could be willing to put in a lot of effort to establish and maintain a good rapport with your boss. Moreover, you might want to try being more open and honest with your manager about your worries and difficulties.

On the other hand, if you have insecure attachment, you might not be as motivated or forthcoming with your employer. Also, you might not be as forthcoming with your coworkers.

Chapter 12:
Steps to Strive Toward Secure Attachment Style

You must start working toward a secure attachment style and abandon your anxious attachment style if you want your relationships to get better because if you do not, you will prevent yourself from finding happiness. It may take months or years to build patterns that resist those old ones, so this job will not be simple because anxious patterns have gotten established in your personality. Yet, if you want to have any chance of having the peaceful, comforting relationships that you probably want, you must make that effort. Even though the complete course of treatment takes a while, you will probably see a difference quite quickly once you start some new habits.

Know What You Are Up Against

Recognize your anxious attachment style before you take any more action. You have probably already identified your attachment style, but you need to do more than just give it a name. You have to be honest with yourself and confess that you have this style and that it has some influence over you. Although it may be difficult to admit that something is in control of your behavior, you must do so if you have any chance of changing it. While it may be in control of you, awareness will give you the power to change it.

The symptoms of anxious attachment can vary from case to case, but you will have a unique set of behaviors that you want to identify. It is time to start thinking critically and assess your anxious attachment tendencies. Do you frequently worry that your partner is cheating on you? Do you worry that your partner will not stay with you because they think you are unworthy? Do you often check up on your partner or peek at their phone without their permission? Do you struggle mightily to hold on to them? You can learn more about your challenges by asking yourself these kinds of questions.

Maintain a journal where you track your progress. Even though many people laugh at the idea of journaling, it is one of the most useful behaviors you can adopt. By keeping a journal, you can better understand your patterns and connect the dots when it might have otherwise taken you longer to do so. Science has shown that keeping a journal is beneficial to your health. According to research, keeping a journal for about fifteen minutes a day for several months can help you feel less stressed. Stress reduction enables you to approach problems more rationally. Also, keeping a journal will enhance your physical health by lowering your risk of illness, sharpening your memory, and improving your mood. Those are just a few of the benefits! Of course, the biggest advantage is that it enables you to gauge your progress and future goals.

Commit to overcoming your anxious attachment. Even though change is often uncomfortable, you must accept it and resolve to give the process your all. If you put out only minimal effort and do not commit because of whatever reservations you may have, you will not experience any rewards and will still find it difficult to maintain healthy relationships. Knowing what you have to deal with will make it simpler for you to commit because you can start to identify key patterns that will affect how you respond to the challenges you encounter.

Reshape Your Thoughts

Your anxiety-inducing thoughts will fight any therapy you try to give them. Cognitive distortions, which are ideas you hold to be true even though your perception is incorrect, are usually produced by your brain as it looks for patterns and tries to make sense of the world using your experiences. For instance, if your parents frequently neglected you, you can develop the unfounded expectation that everyone will treat you in the same way and that they "do not think you are worth the effort of caring" because of prior experiences. You assume the information you have will always be valid, and in the process, you can self-sabotage relationships that defy your cognitive distortion. Cognitive restructuring, a technique that aids in helping you refocus your beliefs, is necessary when dealing with cognitive distortion.

Adopt the ABC approach. Dr. Albert Ellis developed the ABC approach as a model to assist people in understanding the connections between their thoughts, emotions, and actions. It is a strategy that is applied in cognitive-behavioral therapy. For patients to have improved behaviors and mental processes, cognitive-behavioral therapy (CBT) aims to address and rewrite clients' unhelpful thought patterns. The terms "activating event," "beliefs regarding the event," and "consequences of the event" collectively make up the ABC model. The main focus of CBT is the B, which fills in the gaps between A and C. The thought process is activated by an incident, such as your partner not saying hello to you in the morning. The subsequent negative thought patterns brought on by this activating event may lead to negative feelings like hurt, rage, or sadness. In the partner scenario, you may start to believe, "My partner does not love me," based on just that one experience. Then, those anxious thoughts may cause you to feel upset and act out. The consequences are the emotions or behaviors that go along with those beliefs. By breaking down your thought processes using the ABC approach, you can learn to confront your beliefs and stop allowing them to feed your insecurities.

Avoid common thought patterns. Individuals with anxious attachment and other mental disorders tend to fall back on similar thought patterns, which can be more harmful than helpful. You need to identify these patterns and prevent them from happening again. Attempt to change your all-or-nothing mentality. A mistake could feel like the end of the world, but the world has gradients, so it probably is not. There is no absolute right or wrong in every situation, and that is okay. You should not adopt the belief that you are either right or wrong, good or bad, or that you are either winning or losing. Realizing that people can be multiple things at once makes you less judgmental of both yourself and other people. Also, avoid assuming the worst. Even while something horrible could occur, it does not necessarily mean that it will. Slow down and consider what occurred before jumping to the worst possible conclusion. Moreover, avoid making overgeneralizations because they may lead you to feel that certain statements are true regardless of the situation when in fact they are not. It is not a criticism of your cooking abilities if your partner says they do not enjoy what you served for dinner, for instance. One bad meal does not always indicate that you cook poorly every time, and your partner can legitimately dislike the flavors due to their preferences. You must thus be conscious of these tendencies to think in extremes to mediate your thoughts.

Keep an eye on your thought patterns. Acting as a security guard and catching your thought patterns as they enter your head will help you effectively combat them. It does not mean you are safe after you stop thinking in particularly harmful ways. The tendency for negative thought patterns to persist in your mind must be stopped before they develop into ingrained patterns. Recognize when you are over-generalizing or over-simplifying issues, and then constantly remind yourself that your assumptions are incorrect.

Question your presumptions. This technique includes asking plenty of questions about everything. Although it has the potential to be harmful, doubt is thought to be a vital component of faith because blind faith is a flimsy form of belief. Yet if you question and examine it, you either disprove it or the idea just gets stronger. You must test your presumptions and either prove them to be true or untrue to have faith in your relationship that is more than just flimsy. As a result, you should not compromise your relationship's trust to do this assignment. Instead of focusing on what your partner is doing, you should look inside at how you are thinking.

Address Your Shame

Shame is one of the most destructive emotions in anyone's life. Shame is a feeling that results from our bad opinion of ourselves, unlike guilt, which is a feeling based on actions we have committed and hold ourselves accountable for. When people believe they have violated norms or standards that society as a whole holds them to, they experience shame. Shame may be harmful, and studies have shown that people who experience a lot of shame typically have poorer self-esteem.

Researchers Tangney and Dearing also discovered that shame increases a person's risk of developing psychological disorders including depression and substance abuse. Shame is most common in women, although it also affects men and persons who identify as non-binary or transgender. Even though most people experience shame at some point in their life, when that shame persists, it feeds the feelings that cause anxiety. So, it becomes challenging to move on and establish a secure attachment until you deal with your shame.

Find out what makes you feel ashamed, as those are likely the same things that make you anxious in relationships. Differentiate shame from things you need to do better because they are not the same. While there may be some overlap between the two, the things you feel ashamed about relate more to how you feel as a person than they do to whom you aspire to be. Shame does not need to be justified. Because these things do not match what other people expect, many people feel guilty about things they cannot change. As a result, even though you might feel like you need to change the things that make you feel ashamed due to pressure from others, you might only need to alter your mindset. When you change your mindset, you will begin to concentrate more on improving than on feeling worse.

Stop hiding your shame; that is the next thing you should do. You make your shame worse by hiding it. Shame thrives in secrecy. It makes sense that you would not talk about your shame since it makes you feel like there is something wrong with you. Everyone keeps their shame to themselves because they do not want other people to view them in that same way. The shame grows and it develops into a secret that festers and can sever relationships. When you are open and honest about your shame, it loses its power because you are no longer concerned about what other people might think of you if they found out. After all, keeping something to yourself makes you more anxious about how other people may react if they found out.

Address your shame and reframe it. It is critical to face your shame and figure out what you are truly feeling, even if you believe you deserve the guilt you feel. Guilt focuses on your actions and the effects they have on other people, while shame focuses on you as a person even when you have done something wrong. So, it is usually more beneficial to recognize that you are experiencing guilt rather than shame when you feel ashamed. Guilt shifts the conversation and maintains that your acts were terrible, whereas shame will convince you that you are a bad person. When you believe that your actions are inherently wrong, you may feel powerless to change them. But when you come to realize that bad behaviors do not necessarily make you a horrible person, you can address your behaviors and make sure that you perform better behaviors moving forward.

Never let a single experience define who you are as a whole. It does not follow that you are always wrong if you present a bad suggestion during a meeting at work. It is not a sign that you are crazy if your partner declines to participate in an activity with you. You cannot simplify other people or yourself to only a few seconds since people are complex. Your guilt will persuade you that you are completely flawed, but if you can learn to look at things more broadly and overcome your shame, you will begin to realize that you are much more than you currently realize.

Create a Foundation of Self-Esteem

It is simpler to deal with the anxious thoughts that affect your attachment style when you have self-esteem. Although it will not give you a ton of confidence right away, this foundation will help you get started and point you on the right path.

Look for positive aspects about yourself. You should tell yourself five positive things about yourself every day as you look in the mirror. Start with simply one and increase from there if you are unable to name five at this time. Consider your attitude and habits in addition to your outward appearance. What have you performed well? How can you possibly change the world? What part do you play in other people's lives? Everyone has both good and bad attributes, and when you take the time to focus on the positive, you feel better about yourself and are less likely to assume that you are unworthy of other people's love or attention.

Find out what brings you joy. You should only engage in hobbies and recreational activities that you like. Start pondering the things that truly bring you joy. This work appears straightforward, but so many people let their interests go in favor of those of others. Those with low self-esteem are more likely to exhibit this inclination because they frequently try to transform themselves to fit in and win people's affection. Unfortunately, no one can fully come to know them because they mask their true selves. Because nobody knows who they truly are, they can never elicit the feelings they want. They are ashamed and are trying to hide who they are. If you do not drink, for example, you should not feel obligated to go out for drinks with a date! Even if your date enjoys it, if you are not enjoying yourself, they will notice and assume you are not interested in them. Recognize your true interests, even if they are not widely shared.

Pay closer attention to how you use technology. While having a phone, computer, and other technologies is undoubtedly a blessing, they can also hurt your self-esteem, which will make your attachment issues worse. Instagram is the worst social media platform for self-esteem, according to a study of young people by the Royal Society for Public Health. This is probably due to comparison, as well as bullying and shaming that may happen online. The study also found that persons who spent more than two hours on social media were more likely to experience discomfort and mental illness. You do not have to stop using social media and other forms of technology, but being more aware of their impact on your life will improve your self-esteem.

Be ready to adopt new perspectives on the world as you begin to establish a strong sense of self-worth. You will begin to see yourself and other people in a variety of meaningful and novel ways.

Be Merciful With Yourself

If you are not merciful with yourself, goals become difficult to reach, and you will constantly feel as though you are falling short. You must therefore learn to be kinder to yourself. One of the best strategies to change negative thought patterns is to use positive self-talk. When you speak positively, you draw attention to your positive traits. Also, you should learn to own up to your mistakes and realize that they do not necessarily mean failure but rather an opportunity for improvement. Although making errors is never enjoyable, you may learn from them so that you can make wiser choices in the future and improve as a person. Be patient and understand that setbacks are a natural part of the path because you undoubtedly placed a lot of strain on yourself and likely put expectations on relationships. Your inner critic will contest leniency, but you should start being harsh on yourself and keep in mind that nobody is flawless. You should not expect perfection from yourself since you would not expect it from your best buddy. Sometimes the hardest thing you will ever do is forgive yourself, yet doing so is essential for your mental health.

Seek Help

For certain people, more assistance is necessary to overcome their anxious thoughts and develop secure attachment. You can tell that you might require further assistance in several ways. One way is when you feel helpless to deal with your problems on your own. There is a chance that you will encounter complicated problems that require further investigation. You may also need assistance in recognizing and challenging your limiting beliefs. Do not feel ashamed that you cannot manage treatment on your own, regardless of the reason you require more assistance. Find a mental health professional that specializes in the issues you face and be tenacious in seeking help. Try different ones until you find one with whom you click and who appears to comprehend your problems. It might not happen on the first try. Although receiving mental health treatment may appear to be a waste of time or effort, it is an investment in your future and can help you resolve your problems more quickly and safely.

Chapter 13:
Acknowledging Your Anxious Attachment

U nderstanding what is going on in your mind and what might be preventing you from succeeding is vital when trying to make positive changes in your life. This is especially valid if you have anxious attachment.

Understanding Your Anxious Attachment

Many persons with anxious attachments have insecurities about themselves. Because they worry about being rejected or not obtaining what they want, they find it difficult to trust their partner. This makes them appear clingy because it might cause a lot of emotional strain and dissatisfaction in their relationships.

They frequently go to their partner for validation and reassurance, but this seldom allays their ingrained insecurities. These childhood trauma-based fears cause them to worry that their partners would reject them.

Because they can easily become overwhelmed and develop protective feelings, their clinginess might make it challenging for them to be a companion to their kids. This may result in a lack of compassion and understanding for their kids.

The first step you should take if you have an anxious attachment is to recognize and accept your anxieties. Then, make an effort to lessen them by performing calming behaviors, such as talking to yourself positively and seeking support from friends or coworkers.

It may also be necessary for you to set small goals for yourself, such as opening an email that makes you uncomfortable and dedicating just 15 minutes each day to a task that you have put off for several weeks or months. Your confidence and resilience will increase as a result of these small victories, which will make it simpler for you to deal with your anxiety.

It could be challenging to break your life's pattern of anxious attachment. But it is possible if you have patience.

How to Respond to Someone With Anxious Attachment

Anxious attachment is the clingy, insecure style of attachment that frequently results from neglect or abuse as a child. Adult relationships may be affected by this form of attachment, which can lead to issues with closeness, intimacy, and trust.

It might be challenging to know how to react to someone who exhibits an anxious attachment style, but being aware of your attachment style can help you better understand how you interact with others and work toward a more secure relationship.

You can start by recognizing how your actions and interpersonal behaviors are being used as outlets for your anxiety. After you become conscious of these patterns, you can attempt to alter them to improve your emotional well-being and relationships.

By improving your ability to communicate with your partner, you can get over an anxious attachment. This can involve working on gestures and nonverbal communication techniques like posture. This can assist you to understand your partner's needs and feelings as well as help them understand how you feel.

Giving someone with an anxious attachment style constant support is another way to assist them. This may seem straightforward, but it is crucial to keep in mind that anxious people frequently feel overwhelmed by their emotions and lack the skills to manage their strong emotions on their own.

For anxious partners, taking the time to communicate your love and affection can be very beneficial. You should make them know that you are interested in them and will support them no matter what. This will not only provide them comfort in knowing they are loved, but it can also help you learn about their attachment style and how to better satisfy their needs in future relationships.

Regularly express your love and affection to them, especially when they are stressed out or having a bad day. This can be as easy as texting them or giving them a call, but it will demonstrate your interest in them and want to make them feel valued.

If you have an anxious attachment, reassurance is especially important because these people frequently feel uncertain and self-conscious. It can be difficult to express your feelings, but if you are persistent, people will probably notice.

See an emotion-focused therapist if you are having trouble talking with your partner because they can show you how to do it in a way that will make them feel safe and secure. Also, they may teach you how to identify the situations that make you want to react defensively so you can steer clear of them and opt for healthier forms of communication that are more in line with your true needs in a partner.

It is critical to understand that your relationship reflects who you are as a person and how your upbringing has influenced you. Although it is common to have a particular attachment style, your prior experiences can still influence who you are today and how you interact with others.

Why Does Anxiety Attract Avoidants?

Whether you are secure or avoidant, anxiety might seem like an insurmountable relationship challenge. It can be a crippling emotional disorder that makes it difficult for you to lead a fulfilling life. Moreover, it may cause physical symptoms like headaches, insomnia problems, and muscle strain.

A typical and natural response to an immediate threat is anxiety. It is a fight-or-flight response, but it also serves as an adaptive mechanism that enables us to react to dangerous situations in a way that protects our safety and health.

Individuals with anxiety struggle to regulate it, but they can acquire coping mechanisms. They can make an effort to manage their thoughts and feelings, and as a stress-reduction technique, they might turn to yoga or meditation. A mental health expert may also be able to assist them.

Nevertheless, the problem with anxiety is that it might continue even after the threat has subsided. According to psychologist Danielle

Mendes of the Centre for Anxiety and Trauma Disorders at the University of New South Wales in Sydney, this is why moving past it may be so challenging.

It Can Be a Long Road to Recovery

As the underlying wounds that cause anxious feelings are often very deep, healing them may take some time. This may entail dealing with fundamental difficulties from early life as well as changing unhealthy or unsustainable behavioral patterns.

After some time, if your symptoms do not seem to be getting better, it could be time to see a doctor or therapist. They can offer tips on how to deal with your anxiety and assist you in determining what is making it worse.

A GP can refer you to a mental health professional. Treatment for anxiety can take many different forms and may include medication, counseling, or self-help methods like mindfulness.

Numerous things, including stressors in your life like difficult family dynamics or a demanding job, might contribute to anxiety. You may believe that a tragic event from your past is what is making you anxious, or you may have a physical ailment that is to blame.

Long-term anxiety can contribute to other mental health conditions including depression or PTSD. Receiving treatment can help you feel better and put your life back on track.

Exercise, eating well, and having a positive outlook on life are some of the most common ways for lowering anxiety. By enhancing your mood and reducing stress, these techniques help lessen the frequency of your anxiety episodes.

A counselor or therapist can help you deal with your anxiety by providing support and by teaching you coping mechanisms. They can also assist you in figuring out any underlying problems that may be the source of your anxiety.

In addition to helping you deal with any underlying traumas that are causing your symptoms, a qualified therapist or psychologist will be able to offer you guidance and assistance in controlling them. They can also offer advice on selecting the best therapy or other treatments for you.

What Do Anxious Avoidants Want?

Often, people with anxious-avoidant attachment styles have a strong urge to connect with others and seek reassurance in their romantic relationships. They might, however, also be afraid of being unappreciated and shy away from long-term commitments unless they are guaranteed. They may have been ignored or abandoned by their caregivers when they were young, which had an impact on the way they were raised.

They also have a poor view of themselves, which makes them untrusting of others and makes them feel exposed in relationships. When they are in romantic relationships, they could even feel disoriented and confused.

These people often seek casual sexual relationships or "situationships" as a means of gaining intimacy. These relationships might provide people with a lot of comfort, but they can also indicate that they are experiencing anxiety.

Because they cannot be certain that they will receive the intimacy and reassurance they need, these people frequently engage in "situationships" and casual sexual relationships instead of being genuinely committed to a relationship at all.

A rocky relationship may result from this. For those who are predisposed to depression, this may be particularly true.

Understanding how an anxious-avoidant becomes so attached is essential to determining what they want. You may start to heal your attachment wounds and find a fulfilling relationship if you are aware of where they are.

As a kid grows and develops, their attachment patterns are shaped by the care they receive from their parents and other caregivers. For instance, a child who has a secure attachment can rely on their caregiver for both emotional and physical assistance. On the other hand, a child with an anxious-avoidant style will feel the urge to be independent and self-sufficient.

When separated from their caregivers, these children usually behave extremely differently from other children and exhibit symptoms comparable to secure-attached children.

They will be reclusive and may try to exert as much control over their surroundings as they can. Also, they will act very guarded about their territory, refusing to let anyone enter. Unlike secure-attached children, they could struggle to connect with their caregivers and will not be able to express their needs or fears to them.

When they get older, these people typically search for a partner who will be able to meet their needs and who will not be afraid to be intimate with them. Also, they might be a little more likely to commit adultery or engage in sexual activity because doing so can help them feel more secure and close to others. This can be challenging because the type of relationship in question has the potential to significantly affect both your physical and emotional health. It might make you miserable, depressed, or enraged.

Working with a therapist who is skilled in this area, like a certified psychologist or therapist, is the greatest method to mend this kind of relationship. To help you get past it and develop healthier, happier relationships, having a therapist who is familiar with the symptoms of this kind of relationship can make all the difference.

How to Break an Anxious-Avoidant Cycle?

Partners who are anxious and avoidant frequently get stuck in a loop that leaves them feeling as though they have nothing left to give to one another. With time, these patterns may get toxic, making it impossible to maintain the relationship. The first thing to realize about an anxious-avoidant attachment style is that avoidants make up a very small portion of the population. Contrary to what you may anticipate, this kind of attachment style is much more prevalent in relationships.

Several of these individuals had childhood trauma in the past, which made them feel exposed and defenseless. Some people may use their avoidant attachment style as a means of escaping their emotions of loneliness or abandonment.

Contrary to what many anxious attachment specialists would have you believe; avoidant attachment styles can be modified by both partners with the help of mindfulness and self-acceptance practices.

An anxious person can start to alter their behavior and consciously work to increase trust with their partner once they become aware of how their anxiety is hurting them. This could be a crucial step in ending the pattern and creating more intimacy in the relationship.

Communication is another key to ending the cycle with your partner. To better express your needs and desires, you might need to put a few new abilities to use. Using active listening techniques, for instance, can be quite beneficial in communicating your feelings to your partner.

It also entails learning how to have respectful and calm conversations. Although these check-ins might be challenging, they are crucial to mending and preserving your relationship with your avoidant partner.

Being secure usually makes it easier for you to communicate with and understand your partner. Also, you preserve your own identity and have a strong feeling of self-worth outside of the relationship.

By developing more effective and healthier ways to communicate your emotions, you can break the cycle. This means being forthright and honest with your avoidant partner while discussing your feelings.

Addressing any past events that may have influenced your avoidant attachment style is one of the most effective methods to do this. Working with a therapist or other mental health expert can help you explore any earlier traumatic events that may have influenced your current anxiety and avoidance behaviors.

You will gain a better understanding of yourself and your relationship with your avoidant partner as you work through these problems. Also, you will be able to handle disagreements and conflicts with your partner better.

The process of altering your attachment style ultimately takes a lifetime and calls for patience and consistency. Although it could seem difficult, the benefits of a strong relationship are worth the effort!

It is crucial to set aside time to work on your inner healing. As a result, as you mature and become a more secure person, you will probably notice that your avoidant attachment style starts to disappear.

Chapter 14:
Understanding My Triggers

I f you find yourself often acting in a way you do not like, it may be best to consider why this is happening. If your actions are being driven by the needs of others rather than your own needs, then it might be time to face those who trigger these responses from you. Sometimes other people do not even realize they are triggering strong emotional responses from you, and often, these responses can be very much out of proportion with the situation or even with the person.

Techniques to Know What Triggers You

You can use a variety of techniques to increase your awareness of how and why you react the way you do, including:

1. Imagery

Imagery is a technique that allows you to see your negative emotions and feelings. This enables you to reflect on how you are feeling and what those feelings are exactly. It is a terrific method to approach the issue differently, alter your point of view, and develop problem-solving skills in emotional or stressful situations. It can be challenging to understand what is wrong with you or why you feel so overwhelmed during a panic or anxiety episode. By using imagery, you may make sense of the situation and realize that it is okay to feel overwhelmed.

How to do this?

Step 1.   Create an image of what you are feeling.

Step 2.   Describe the feelings that you are experiencing.

Step 3.   Name the emotions, like anxiety or stress.

Step 4.   Determine where in your body you can feel them.

Step 5.   Repeat the process if necessary.

2. Journaling

Journaling is a great way to understand your emotions. It is a technique for looking back on your life and figuring out what makes you feel the way you do.

How to do this?

Step 1.   Get a journal.

Step 2.   Sit down somewhere private and quiet.

Step 3.   Write freely.

Step 4.   Learn from the written entries.

Step 5.   Remember your emotions.

3. Talking to someone

Communicating with others is a straightforward and effective method for understanding and connecting with your emotions. You can talk about your feelings with a friend, your partner, or even your family. Speak to someone who is great at spending time with you and who also listens intently to what you have to say without interrupting or passing judgment. It is essential to have a sympathetic and understanding person. They will understand what it is like for you, how it feels, why it happens, and what goes along with these feelings to a greater extent if they are more aware of how you feel. Communicating to someone in this manner will improve their listening abilities, and because they are concerned about your feelings, they could listen attentively to comprehend them more fully.

Talking to someone is different from just sharing your feelings, though, because when you talk to someone, you are actively attempting to change things. You are trying to make them understand how you feel so that the next time you mention these feelings, you will not get the same reaction. You can understand why something feels so off by conversing with others. Instead of merely accepting things as they are, figure out what is the root of your emotional issues and attempt to address them. Do not be discouraged if the person you are speaking to does not grasp what you are saying; this could be your chance to discover someone who will listen and provide you with new solutions to these problems.

4. Talk to a professional

Finding the triggers may need the assistance of a qualified healthcare professional because some of them may be obscure. Many psychiatrists and psychologists focus on difficulties relating to emotions. They can truly help you over the phone or in person to achieve a state of calm.

Things to Consider when choosing a psychologist

1. Your belief system: To undertake therapy with a psychologist, it is important that you feel comfortable talking about certain things with them. Therapy is not always effective, and some individuals may find it difficult to disclose certain experiences

and emotions in the presence of a therapist. But, for them to properly understand your experiences, the therapist needs to come from a similar background to you.

2. Issues that may arise: You should also consider whether you can speak with the psychotherapist without getting upset. It is critical to choose a therapist who can adapt to new issues as they arise. Knowing that the therapist has a plan of action in case things get challenging can help you keep calm and not feel anxious about going into detail during sessions. Also, a good therapist should be able to gather information without compromising your privacy, allowing you to feel comfortable discussing openly these problems with them.

3. Location: You also need to consider the difficulty in traveling to your chosen therapist, as any distance will make it difficult for a regular conversation. If you can travel, this can be advantageous as it allows you to meet the psychotherapist in person, allowing for a more comfortable and personal relationship. If traveling is not an option, find out when they are at the office so that you can schedule your calls around those times.

4. Fees: To avoid being surprised by a bill at the end of therapy sessions, you must be aware of the fees upfront. Make sure you are aware of any possible additional fees, such as those that might apply if you decide to keep seeing the therapist after a certain period. It is always a good idea to be aware of the prices so you are not taken aback by a huge bill at the end.

5. Guarantee: When looking for a therapist, it is crucial to inquire about any guarantees. This means that if your personal issues start to get worse at some point in therapy, then you will be able to seek help from that particular psychotherapist again. Following your initial session, insurance companies often guarantee therapists for a certain period. This guarantee may aid you in determining whether or not the therapist is the perfect fit for you.

6. Speaking with a stranger will give you the freedom to reveal your hidden emotions without worrying about being judged. They can also help you deal with these emotions from different angles, spark original thoughts you had not considered before, and offer support when you need it most.

7. Emotions are incredibly simple to experience but often difficult to comprehend. It might be challenging to get along with other people when you first begin to feel emotionally invested in particular issues. These emotions might appear out of nowhere, and no matter how hard you attempt to dismiss them, they persist. These emotions not only aggravate interactions with others but also put a strain on you. To learn how to handle these feelings, it is crucial that you understand what is producing them.

We interact with others daily and experience emotions, often without recognizing how painful they can be. We need to be taught about the many emotions we feel and the reasons behind them, which is one of the key issues with emotions. Without being able to explain why certain emotions are present, we start to link them to a particular scenario or event. If given the chance, you can identify a wide range of emotions in both yourself and other people. You will observe a variety of emotions, such as happiness, sadness, mistrust, or jealousy. To better manage your life and reduce the burden on those around you, learn how to manage your emotions.

Chapter 15:
Learn to Let Go of Your Anxious Attachment

W hen left alone by our partners, the majority of us frequently experience anxiety. By letting go of the anxious attachment, you can get rid of this feeling. Giving up the anxious attachment entails ceasing to analyze your partner's every move and decision. It means allowing them some time apart from you without feeling guilty or at fault. It also necessitates that you have a basic awareness of the fact that everyone has a different way of being.

It takes practice, so do not expect to be able to let go of the anxious attachment right away. Remind yourself frequently that when you grasp on closely to your partner, you are also tying them to you. This will make it challenging for them to leave you if they decide to do so.

You must be aware that letting go of the anxious attachment could result in your partner leaving you. This makes sense and is normal. Knowing when to let go and when to cling on tightly is what love is all about. So instead of holding on even harder in your relationship, try practicing letting go a little bit each day.

Keep in mind that giving up on your partner does not mean letting go of the anxious attachment. It merely entails letting go of your anxiety regarding how they would behave in the relationship. It implies altering how you interact with them. You must comprehend their particular traits, motivations, views, and worries to do this.

You must also be aware that some people are more adept than others at letting go of anxious attachment. They may have never relied on anybody else. They may have always been independent and find it difficult to understand why you need someone else to make you happy.

To discover love again, you must be prepared to put in a lot of effort to let go of the anxious attachment. You must regain your ability to trust, believe in, and unquestioningly support others. You must learn to let go of your immature idea that you always have control over things. It is best to stop trying to control things, break free from your anxiety attachment, and learn to let go if you want to be able to love again.

Six Steps to Move Beyond Anxious Attachment

As we become older, we start to notice things about our parents and other significant adults in our lives. Even while they could have a great impact on our life, these people might also make us exhibit anxious attachment responses.

Step 1. Recognize your thoughts, feelings, and actions.

Provide a brief description of how you may be feeling, thinking, or behaving in a given situation. For instance, if you believe someone is avoiding you or withholding their affection, or if you cannot sleep because of relationship concerns.

Recognize your ideas and feelings, then pay attention to how you are reacting to them. Then, imagine what might be happening and how it might impact you. Think about your past experiences with anxious attachment and how they impacted your life.

Step 2. Acknowledge the problem.

Ask yourself what might be causing your thoughts, feelings, and behaviors. If you have concerns about a person or situation, consider how those concerns may be influencing you and whether you may be overreacting.

Step 3. Focus on what is relevant.

Take note of the relevant details of the problem and search for possible solutions. Consider what is happening and how you might handle the situation rather than dwelling on your concerns or anxiety.

You will be better able to work through anxious attachment and build a secure relationship — or just avoid anxious attachment entirely — if you concentrate on what is important and try to fix problems as they come up.

Step 4. Start with what you can control.

This phase serves as a helpful reminder that, despite your concerns about the other person, the only thing you have control over is how you react to the situation. You can feel more in control of the situation if you concentrate on your behaviors and reactions.

Step 5. Use your skills to overcome your fear.

Concentrate on the facts you already know and can trust. The more knowledgeable you are in a particular area, the less likely it is that you will make a mistake or poor decision. For instance, you will rarely smash into a wall once you learn how to ride a bike.

Consider any knowledge or abilities you already possess that could aid in overcoming your fear and anxiety. Consider tactics you can use to feel more at ease speaking in front of a group of people, for instance, if you are anxious about public speaking.

Step 6. Take action.

After considering your go-to strategy for handling the situation, try coming up with a new way.

When you commit to this new behavior, keep an eye on your anxiety levels. You will probably be able to utilize this strategy again if they stop and you have tried something else. Practice overcoming your anxiety if the problem persists or worsens over time.

How Do You Move Past the Struggle?

Letting go of your anxious attachment is hard work, but it will undoubtedly offer advantages. If you truly want to let go and regain your trust, start this process cautiously and practice letting go a little bit each day. If your past experiences have made you believe that letting go is impossible, consider them as lessons that will help you achieve your goals in terms of love and relationships.

You might need to let your ex-partners off the hook for everything they did wrong. Even if you cannot forgive them, accepting what happened in the past and letting go of any animosity will make it simpler for you to let go of your anxious attachment. Remember, you should forgive both yourself and others if you want to go on.

It is also helpful if you can teach someone else how to let go. Develop the skill of letting go of the things you have been holding on to for a very long time. Begin by granting yourself forgiveness and acquiring the ability to let go. You will soon lose the anxiety attachment, feeling lighter and happier.

The best way to assist yourself in letting go of the anxious attachment is to practice self-acceptance and self-love. Before you can love another person, you first need to value your existence. The more self-love you possess, the less hesitant you will be to open yourself to others. After that, it will be simpler for you to let go of the anxious attachment.

You will gain more self-confidence if you let go of your anxious attachment. This will assist you in developing new relationships and trusting yourself and others. Also, you will develop an open mind to other people's perspectives and allow them to express themselves without bias or prejudice. You have stopped clinging to negativity, so it is simple for you to get past any bad experiences or relationships with others.

You could notice that letting go of the anxious attachment necessitates some lifestyle changes. You might need to change the people you hang out with, how you work, and how you spend your time. As soon as you begin this practice, you will go through a journey of discovery.

As a result of having to solve your difficulties without assistance from others, you could initially feel alone. It is a fantastic chance for non-threatening self-reflection and self-discovery. You will be completely alone at this point, but you will still be able to take on this issue on your own because you have no one or nothing to rely on.

What Feelings Will Come Up When You Are Moving Forward?

Going forward is a difficult task that initially may seem overwhelming. The first baby step toward a new relationship is where it all begins. Moving forward, you have mixed emotions of anxiety, optimism, and exhilaration. While you scan the horizon for what is coming up, you can feel anxious. It is crucial to carry on along this route in search of a new relationship, new career, new friend, or new hobby even though you are hesitant to do so. You gain experience by moving forward more frequently.

Going forward entails exposing yourself to life's "unknowns." This is the scary part. There is nothing to fear even if you cannot predict what will happen next if you have the power to manage it. You can only learn about yourself and get experience from it.

Make sure to immediately request assistance if you require it. Make an effort to discuss your current situation with someone else. Also, it will help you build stronger relationships with others.

You feel at ease talking openly about what is going on in your life when you can be honest with yourself. Both from others and yourself, you have nothing to conceal. This is the secret to making decisions that improve your life and your relationships. Also, having this sense of integrity will make you more appealing to others.

You must believe that you are in charge of your life and the decisions you make. Most people who are anxious do not experience this healthy sense of control. Because they adopt this unhealthy behavior to make themselves feel better about themselves, they continue living this unhealthy lifestyle.

You must consider how your decisions impact both you and those around you. Letting go of the anxious attachment is a significant step. There is less chance that you will harm someone else when you can make judgments based on how they will impact others. For those who are overcome with fear, this is difficult. But you truly do not want to hurt others, do you? Always keep in mind that your anxiety attachment will start to lessen the more honest you are with yourself and others.

Chapter 16:
Overcoming Negative Interactions

P eople can have negative thoughts for a variety of reasons including depression or low self-esteem. But there are also powerful strategies for getting rid of unfavorable thoughts and shifting to a more optimistic mindset.

Start by recognizing the negative influences in your life and replacing them with positive ones. The individuals you spend time with, websites, music, and other things that make you feel bad could all fall under this category.

Use mindfulness meditation and pay attention to your thoughts to determine when they are negative. You can even do this at the end of the day to take a moment to appreciate all that has gone right for you that day.

By making an effort to see the good in everything in your life, you can develop a positive mindset and strong emotional foundation. This can be challenging at first, but if you persevere, you will notice a change in your attitude and focus toward positivity.

Recognize and detect destructive thought processes including labeling, overgeneralizing, and catastrophizing. As you recognize these practices, challenge them by questioning your thought patterns and reshaping your ideas to be more realistic.

Stop the Negative Thoughts Before They Become a Problem

Stopping negative thinking before it has a chance to negatively impact your daily life is one of the most effective methods for doing so. You may stop negative ideas before they take over your mind and skew your vision by becoming aware of when they are not neutral or factual.

As soon as you detect any negative thoughts, write them down. Writing down your thoughts will help you recognize that, despite how difficult it may initially seem, these emotions are real and manageable.

Reach Out for Support

It can be easier to deal with negative thoughts if you can talk about them with a friend or member of your family. If you express your feelings to someone you trust, you will also feel more understood.

Maintain a journal and record your thoughts as they come to you. Writing down your thoughts can enable you to understand what is going through your mind and will offer you the chance to reinterpret them more positively.

Avoid those who are negative or who continuously criticize you since they can make your thoughts lean that way. These individuals could be close to you, like your parents, friends, or coworkers, but they could also be distant, like internet acquaintances or famous people.

A mental health professional should be consulted if you are experiencing a pattern of persistently unpleasant thoughts that are affecting your quality of life. This will give you the chance to decompress, locate the root of your skewed ideas and negative thoughts, and work on finding solutions in a safe setting.

Ways to Overcome Negative Thinking

Everyone occasionally has negative thoughts, but for some people, they can be a recurring issue. Whichever level of negativity you have experienced, there are some simple measures you can do to get rid of it and live a better life.

1. **Make a conscious effort to catch negative thoughts as they creep in.**

Negative thoughts can be quite painful, and they often give the impression that they are going to prevail. But being conscious of these thoughts as they enter your head and responding to them directly can help you overcome them. This can be done in a variety of ways, such as saying to yourself aloud to reaffirm that you do not feel as horrible as you may be feeling inside, focusing on your shoes or clothing when you start to think about how you appear, or both.

2. **Change your environment to get out of the situation that you are in and think about something different.**

If you are struggling to deal with the stress of your negative thoughts, getting out of the situation can help you move past them. A walk or even just sitting on a park bench can help you shift your perspective and discover something more uplifting to concentrate on.

3. **Practice mindfulness and breathe deeply.**

Deep breathing will help you focus on the present moment, which is typically where unfavorable thoughts emerge. Those who experience anxiety or depression can benefit the most from this practice since it can help them feel relieved and concentrate on the here and now.

4. Make a joke about the situation at hand.

Although it might be challenging, laughing at our negative thoughts is a practice that can help us change them. It is a terrific technique to utilize with family members and friends who could be thinking negatively.

5. Stop allowing negative thoughts to hang around for too long and set a timer.

An extremely powerful method for overcoming the habit of harboring negative ideas in your head is to set a timer for no more than one minute. You can do this by setting a timer on your smartphone and reminding yourself not to open the door for them after the minute is up.

6. Keep a positive self-talk diary or thought journal.

Thought journals are a great tool for assisting in the identification of negative thinking patterns and can be used in conjunction with cognitive behavioral therapy (CBT). Also, they will teach you how emotions like anger and sadness may be brought on by your thoughts, which will allow you to practice controlling your emotions.

It can be difficult to overcome the habit of thinking negatively, but the effort is worthwhile. In the long term, it will improve your mood and release your potential. The suggestions above are a fantastic place to start, but it is crucial that you seek out mental health assistance if your negative thought patterns have become ingrained or if they are interfering with your day-to-day life.

Chapter 17:
Improve Your Self-Confidence and Self-Esteem

S uccess in life depends on one's ability to feel confident. It can lessen stress, improve your relationships, and open you up to new experiences. It can also make your dreams come true and give you the confidence to express yourself.

Having confidence can take many different shapes and differ from person to person. While some people exude confidence naturally, others require a little more effort. This is why it is crucial to invest the necessary time in boosting your self-confidence and learning the skills that will enable you to feel more confident in general. Practice these tips to increase your self-confidence:

1. Identify your core values and passions.

Understanding your passions and values can help you make wise decisions in life, which is crucial for boosting self-confidence. Also, it might help you set goals and strive toward them.

2. Keep a gratitude journal to remember your favorite things.

A great way to keep your mind on the positive aspects of your life and boost your confidence by concentrating on what matters is to write down what you are grateful for. It is a great method to keep track of your accomplishments and acknowledge the positive changes in your life.

3. Stop negative self-talk.

Making harsh remarks about yourself and other people is one of the easiest ways to lose self-confidence. This happens frequently, especially when you are depressed or insecure. Saying "I am no good," or "I cannot do this," is a common pitfall. The issue with this is that these ideas just serve to undermine your self-confidence and are harmful in many other aspects of your life.

4. Think about your best self.

Having a positive body image might help boost your confidence. Understanding that everybody is unique and that everyone has strengths and weaknesses is crucial. The secret to having a positive body image is to value and celebrate the aspects of your physical appearance that you find appealing.

5. Set small goals and attain them.

Setting goals is a crucial component of boosting your self-confidence, whether you are aiming to get in shape or learn how to cook. Smaller, more manageable goals make them simpler to accomplish and can offer you the confidence you need to be successful.

6. Push your comfort zone.

Although it can be frightening, taking risks is crucial to developing your confidence. Sometimes it is a good idea to push yourself and occasionally try something terrifying, like skydiving or bungee jumping. Even if you are unsuccessful, you will have gained insight into who you are which will increase your confidence moving forward.

7. Develop a more positive body image.

By enabling you to perceive yourself as a whole person rather than just the parts you dislike, a positive body image can aid in the development of your self-confidence. It is a great way to motivate yourself to work out and eat well. By developing a positive body image, you will be less likely to compare your look to that of others and more inclined to recognize that people of all sizes and shapes have a place in the world.

Ways to Build Your Self-Confidence

1. Build your self-confidence by taking action.

The best way to increase your confidence is to make progress toward your goals and objectives, even if those efforts appear insignificant at first. This shows that you can get through the fears and concerns that come with trying anything new, and it aids in changing your negative thought patterns.

2. Prepare for every challenge.

Practicing may help you become more confident in stressful situations, whether it is delivering a presentation to your boss or giving a speech to a huge audience. You can practice your skills and be ready for whatever may arise when you have a lot of preparation time before the event.

3. Learn from your failures.

Confident people are aware that failures and mistakes are crucial components of learning. They perceive them as possibilities for growth and improvement rather than as indicators that they are acting improperly.

4. Be committed to your goals and objectives.

Those who are successful dedicate themselves to their goals and strive arduously to realize them. They are more inclined to persevere when things are difficult because they think they deserve the best and will not accept anything less than their full potential.

5. Take care of yourself.

If you lack confidence, it could be because you do not think you are doing enough to maintain your overall health and well-being. Poor eating habits, a lack of exercise, or concern for what other people think can all contribute to this.

6. Focus on your successes.

Making a list of all the positive things you accomplish in life, such as achieving an A on an exam or mastering bike riding, can boost your self-esteem and confidence. Then, you can keep a list of these accomplishments and refer to it whenever you are having trouble finding the drive to begin your next major endeavor or complete a long-standing goal.

7. Look for the positives in others.

Being helpful and motivating to others is one of the best methods to increase your self-confidence. This can be achieved by observing other people's positive traits and then praising them for them.

8. Make eye contact.

Many people find it difficult to look others in the eye when they speak to them, so make it a habit to smile and look other people in the eye whenever you can. It is a simple change, but once it becomes ingrained in your routine, it can significantly boost your sense of confidence.

Strong self-confidence can increase your happiness, life satisfaction, and willingness to attempt new things. Even more job happiness and increased productivity may result from it.

Keys to Self-Esteem

Self-esteem is the degree of confidence you have in your abilities and personal worth. Your motivation and mental health are impacted, and your life may be positively or negatively affected. Finding the correct balance depends on understanding your unique self-esteem.

Having healthy self-esteem means you feel confident about yourself and your abilities. This enduring perception of your abilities and characteristics can be a key factor in long-term outcomes, such as happiness, success, and relationships.

- You believe that you have a place in the world: People with high self-esteem are aware of their importance, worth, and deservingness of others' love and respect. They do not permit unjust or exploitative treatment of them.
- You take risks more courageously: People with high self-esteem are less likely to be afraid of failing and to have unrealistic expectations of themselves. They also do not get frustrated or

disappointed when they fail to accomplish a goal they set for themselves.

- Your body is important: A strong sense of self-esteem can lead to self-care practices that promote happiness, health, and comfort. This entails maintaining a healthy diet, exercising frequently, and juggling your obligations to your friends, family, and job.

- You can take control of your thoughts and beliefs: Although your beliefs have great power, you do not have to let them dictate how you live. Instead, consciously try to become aware of and alter your automatic thoughts. By doing this, you will have more control over your thoughts and emotions around the circumstances that undermine your self-esteem. You will come to recognize them for what they are, and you can alter your perspective to be more neutral or favorable.

- The icy blast of your morning shower: Although forcing oneself to suffer a painful shower first thing in the morning may seem like an odd way to start your day, it is one of the best ways to build discipline.

- Practicing meditation and other self-reflection techniques: Being aware of your thoughts can help build a more positive outlook on life. This routine can lift your spirits and give you more energy while lowering anxiety and stress.

- You are open to feedback: If you have a high sense of self-esteem, you may be open with yourself and seek out other people's opinions. This aids in your development and growth.

- Your relationships are positive: Having healthy self-esteem enables you to be more receptive to helpful criticism from friends and relatives. This allows you the chance to hone your skills and strengthen your areas of weakness, which can help your relationships.

Though it is not always simple, it is not impossible to maintain high self-esteem. Improved relationships, a better job, and greater overall well-being can result from taking action to boost your self-image and sense of confidence.

Ways to Improve Your Self-Esteem

Whatever your level of confidence or self-esteem, there are numerous things you can do to make things better. But keep in mind that every person has different things that work for them at different times.

1. Make a list of the things you love about yourself.

By doing this, you can identify some of the things that are significant to you and learn how to concentrate your efforts on them when you are feeling down. You might feel better about yourself and be more motivated to move forward in life as a result.

2. Celebrate your small victories.

You can spend so much time trying to solve all of your issues that you forget to be grateful for the positive aspects of your life. Therefore, be sure to set aside time to recognize the little accomplishments, such as a new talent you have picked up or a job well done.

3. Do not be afraid to try something new.

People with low self-esteem frequently shy away from opportunities and challenges, primarily because they are worried about failing. But, venturing outside of your comfort zone can boost your confidence and demonstrate that you are capable of achieving your goals.

4. Set goals for yourself.

Setting goals that are both realistic and attainable is a great way to boost your self-esteem. For instance, if you want to start exercising frequently, commit to doing a few exercises each day for a week.

5. Stop using negative self-talk.

Low self-esteem is frequently caused by negative self-talk, which can be challenging to modify. Your mental health may suffer if you are continuously telling yourself that you are not good enough or that nothing nice will ever happen to you. Depression and anxiety may result.

6. Talk to someone about it.

Speaking with a therapist might be a helpful strategy to boost your self-esteem if you are experiencing low self-esteem. The therapist can assist you in developing a fresh perspective on the issue and in identifying potential solutions.

7. Surround yourself with supportive people.

Your self-esteem can be greatly impacted by being around uplifting, supportive individuals. It is simple to get caught up in a vicious cycle if your friends and family do not support you.

8. Be mindful of your thoughts and beliefs.

Using mindfulness and meditation techniques can be beneficial if you catch yourself thinking negatively. By doing this, you can get the awareness necessary to separate yourself from your thoughts and beliefs.

9. Do not be afraid to try something new.

Trying something new, whether it is an activity or an entirely different way of looking at life, is a great method to boost your confidence. The only way to determine whether you have what it takes is to do it, which can be frightening.

Chapter 18:
Reforming Your Attachment Style

You are likely aware of how pervasive an anxious attachment style may be in your life if you have read about it or have personally experienced it. Researchers assert that although some people are predisposed to particular relationship attachments based on early experiences, their attachment style may be more flexible than they first thought. Also, depending on your personality and that of your partner, attachment can change during the course of a relationship. Hence, even while numerous factors can support some of your anxious attachment behaviors, you can also use these factors to reduce your relationship insecurity and deepen your ties to the people you care about.

Know Your Signposts

You must become aware of what signposts mark your relationship anxiety and learn how to reroute yourself in healthy directions. According to research, those who lack secure attachment styles frequently have trouble managing their emotions. You struggle to open yourself up to others when you cannot control your emotions, which leads to intimacy problems. You can stop yourself when you start to feel anxious about your actions and feel your blood start to heat up. Learn the symptoms of relationship insecurity so that you can prevent your emotions from controlling you. Relationship insecurity never appears out of nowhere.

Consider the traumatic experience that helped to mold you and how it continues to affect your life. Trauma is the scar you bear as a result of painful events and the tool you use to try to protect yourself from additional harm. There is a good likelihood that a traumatic event you went through as a child contributed to your insecure attachment style. Even while you might claim, "My childhood was not terrible, so I do not have trauma," many people do have trauma that is not addressed. Even if you had a pleasant childhood overall, even minor incidents that made you feel unsafe or hated might have a lasting effect. Even when your parents' critiques were motivated by a desire to keep you safe, it can nevertheless make you feel unworthy if they happen frequently.

Recognize the early signs of anxiety. Every time a person experiences anxiety, a pattern often emerges. For example, it might begin as a dull twisting in your stomach and then develop into trembling hands, perspiration in the armpits, and fury. So, it is beneficial to keep track of how you handle anxiety in your relationship. You can gain a better understanding of how your anxiety works by journaling. You will have a better understanding of your triggers as you jot down as many facts as you can, and you will begin to recognize clues that you previously missed. Even while not every circumstance will follow the same pattern, you may usually avoid difficulties by using your usual patterns.

When you can recognize when insecurity first arises, you can eliminate it before it gets out of control. You start to control your anxiety rather than allowing it to control you. Fighting your anxiety can be frightening, but as you get closer to it, you will notice that it appears to be much bigger than it is. Understanding yourself gives you the ability to anticipate your reactions and practice having different reactions. Bad habits are difficult to overcome, especially reactions you have had for a long time. Yet, if you practice new behaviors over time, the old ones will ultimately disappear and cease to be your default actions.

Consider Your Amygdala

Your brain's amygdala is the area responsible for managing emotional memories. Understanding your amygdala can therefore help you get back on track when you start to feel lost when you are having to create a secure attachment because of your prior wounds. The amygdala struggles with gradient thinking. Instead, it detects either if you are in danger or not. "I might be in danger, but I am not likely to get hurt," is not an option. The amygdala will use your previous responses and experiences to mold how you currently respond. It reacts as rapidly as it can because timing can mean the difference between life and death. Try to recognize the reasons behind your feelings of panic or threat as they arise. Consider how your early experiences shaped the instinctive reactions you have today. When you are conscious, you can begin to question the assumptions your amygdala makes and you can retrain your brain by making deliberate efforts to confront the thought processes that jeopardize the security of your relationships.

Your Feelings Are Important, but They Are Skewed

Although feelings should never be taken lightly, they do not always accurately reflect reality. You need to understand that even while what you are feeling could seem very genuine, taking a step back might help you realize that reality is often a lot more complex than your initial perceptions. Your perspective will always be constrained, so what you think of your partner might not reflect what they think of you. Because of your prior experiences, you might think that your partner feels a certain way, but until you ask them about their feelings, you can never be sure of their interpretation of a situation. Although someone appears to be furious with you in an explicit way, they can feel hurt, disappointed, or angry for reasons unrelated to you since people do not always react in the ways that you expect. When you notice your partner seems strange, it is easy to start worrying. While it is important to pay attention to your emotions, you should not act on them until you have done some investigation and come to a more complete understanding.

Contemplate Your Personality

The way your insecurity in a relationship manifests depends on your personality and tendencies; for instance, if you are passive, you might be passive-aggressive, or if you are confrontational, you might yell when you are stressed. Whatever your personality is like, there are aspects of it that will show when you start to feel anxious and leave a bad impression. You become moodier and less able to control your impulses when you are anxious about a relationship, which makes it more likely that you will act on your impulses rather than stop to think things through. Understanding your personality will help you not only cut down on the number of destructive behaviors you engage in but also teach you how to make the most of your positive personality qualities to improve relationships and communication.

You cannot change your personality traits or skills because they are inborn components of who you are, but you can learn to enhance your greatest qualities. Try to employ aspects of your personality that promote better communication when you want to lash out. For instance, if you naturally tell stories and are a skilled writer, writing may be the best form of communication for you. You might then convey your problems or concerns in writing to your partner. Another example would be that if you are organized, you could utilize that quality to take a moment to gather your thoughts before acting impulsively, or you could plan a meeting with your partner to work out some of the problems you are having. You can use a variety of original strategies to boost your communication and encourage a more secure attachment style.

Think of Your Partner's Tendencies

Your partner will typically handle particular situations in a specific way since they have their unique attachment style. Start paying attention to how your partner handles their worries, then think of ways you may show greater restraint in the future. You should try to remember that your partner also has insecurities and that the greatest way to persuade them to open up is by being helpful rather than defensive. You need to be more accepting of your partner's inclinations and learn to work with them rather than against them because no human will ever be flawless at conveying their wants and understanding their partner's needs. While you cannot change your partner's key characteristics, you may encourage a healthier use of those characteristics.

Learn to Heal Your Inner Child

Every one of us has a wounded child inside. That child has heart wounds, and they anticipate that they will only experience more wounds in the future. As a result, they try to shield themselves from harm, but in doing so, they lose sight of the light. They become stuck in the darkness and long to escape, yet they remain there out of fear for the perils that await them in the light. You are unable to forget the inner child whom someone injured at no fault of the child. Consider your childhood, and demonstrate to the child that their dreams can come true. Make it clear to them that they do not need to be terrified. Offer them the compassion and support they need to move past their wounds and learn to become happier, more confident adults.

Visualize Secure Attachment

Your chances of achieving your goals in the future rise when you develop your visualization skills. According to research, your brain absorbs up to 90% of its information visually. Also, the processing speed of visual information by the brain is substantially faster than that of other inputs. For instance, it can sort through visual information 60,000 times faster than word information, according to the University of Minnesota! So, when you can visualize what you want to happen, your brain is more open to that information and you can feed your subconscious with your hopes as opposed to allowing negativity to shape your unconscious behaviors and thought patterns. Visualizing things helps you develop a mentality that supports a more secure attachment style.

Think about being in a relationship where you are not anxious. Even if you want to be above the surface, breathing easily, when you have an insecure attachment style, it feels as though something is forcing you underwater. You try to get outside, but the weight of your worries prevents you. Imagine yourself now breaking through the water. Without being concerned about the day you will be back underwater, you can swim, laugh, and interact with your partner. Your life is easier, and your relationship does not feel like a fight for your survival. You may remind yourself of what you desire and how you will feel when you have it by visualizing the freedom you can have in the future.

Because there are so many promising relationships out there waiting for you, allow yourself to feel optimistic about the future. Your internal uncertainty just serves to paint a negative picture of the future, but you can get rid of that picture and replace it with one you would prefer to have. As you continue to develop your relationship, utilize what you have imagined to check in on how you and your partner are doing. Consider what you want to see in a relationship and how you want your partner to treat you. Adapt your visualization as necessary to take into account your changing wants and needs. Take things as they come and be free to daydream about a better future since what is good for you right now will not be good for you later.

Remember the Good Instead of the Bad

Keep in mind your partner's positive traits because it is these traits that serve as a reminder of why you should make the effort to be with them. It is simple to make a long list of all the things in your partner that irritate you and conclude that they must not love you as much as you do. Try to come up with a list of all the positive ways your relationship affects you rather than concluding that negative one. When do they boost your self-confidence? In what ways do they support your individuality? How do they contribute to your interests which are mostly foreign to them? What is it about them that makes you smile? You will be able to recognize how your partner loves you through the answers to these questions. And with all that in mind, the more you rewrite the negative conversation with yourself, the more you will feel better about their intentions.

You ought to keep in mind your positive qualities. Do not continue to think things like, "I am always the problem. I'll never be liked by anyone since I can never do anything well." That kind of thinking is counterproductive because it makes you want to react violently to any minor issue. Spend some time every day reflecting on your best qualities as a partner. How do you show your partner that you care? How do you assist them in becoming a better version of themselves? What actions do you think they would value the most? What small acts of kindness do you perform every day? What is it that you most want to share with them that you have kept to yourself? These questions help you become more self-aware and help you recognize how you contribute to the relationship.

Recognize that both you and your partner have positive and negative aspects. Although these components have the potential to be disastrous, many people use them to foster closer bonds. Your partner can strengthen your weaknesses while you can use their strengths to mitigate the effects of their weaknesses. The fun of working in a team is that you receive what makes the other person great while without losing what makes you great individually! You must accept both your partner's and your strengths and weaknesses if you want to develop a secure attachment style.

Know That Each Relationship Is Different

Avoid comparing your relationships too much because each one will have different difficulties and hurdles. Secure attachment will look different in each relationship. When you replace one of those initial partners with a new one, what encourages security in one set of partners might alter. Depending on your personality and who has what attachment style, these variables may alter! Use the knowledge you have gained from previous relationships, but keep in mind that every relationship will come with its own set of difficulties. Because it is impossible to perceive a situation in its entirety, treating each relationship as if it were the same fosters the insecure attachment with the reasoning that "Oh, that is what happened before, so that must be what is happening now."

Never Sacrifice Yourself

Adhere to your values. Your values are a core component of who you are, and they are not likely to change. Many people find meaning in their values, so if you attempt to change them to please another person, you are sacrificing yourself. You will constantly feel imprisoned in an insecure relationship if someone cannot embrace your values. While it would be wonderful to think that any relationship can succeed with enough effort, it is just not true. Some relationships will not ever make you feel comfortable, either because you and your partner have different underlying values or because your partner will not acknowledge your needs and make an effort to meet them. Thus, you must determine whether being in a relationship requires sacrificing yourself. If the answer is yes, strive to make the necessary adjustments, which frequently succeed. You might need to break up with someone if trying to right the situation does not work.

Keep yourself from being engrossed with the other person. You can prevent allowing the other person's identity to dominate how you define yourself by setting clear boundaries and staying true to yourself. The line between you and the other person needs to be clear in your mind. Although there will be a lot of overlap in your life, it is still important to be aware of your boundaries. For instance, many couples who live together and have been dating for a while share bank accounts. If this is something you find uncomfortable, you can set a boundary. Setting a boundary does not imply that you do not trust the other person; rather, it indicates the level of independence you require to feel safe. By treating your insecure attachment, you can work up to having a bank account, but you can do so at your own pace (or not at all). You will trust your partner more and have fewer worries about the relationship when they respect your boundaries.

Never hurt yourself in the name of hurting someone else. Passive aggression can appear to be more convenient than confrontation, but because it sidesteps the real problems, it damages your relationship and breeds more insecurity. Many passive-aggressive individuals engage in actions that harm them more than anyone else. It may feel momentarily good to be passive-aggressive, but it does not allay your fears. Until something else occurs that causes them to resurface, all of those concerns are still present but compressed down and disregarded. The longer you put off worrying, the more compact they get, and whenever they finally surface, they are stronger than ever.

You do not need to prove your value to anyone, including yourself. You are worthy simply for being human. You have good in you, and you have something that someone will appreciate. The ability to be a decent companion for someone else should not ever need you to pass any tests. If someone does not immediately see your value, they are not treating you in a way that will ever result in a stable relationship. You need to find someone who accepts you as you are right away; otherwise, you will feel like you have to constantly prove yourself throughout the relationship and will not be able to find peace.

Instead of needing someone else to save you, learn to save yourself. A common fantasy of many people is that the person they are dating will take care of all their problems. They believe, "I will not worry again if I can discover the ideal partner for me." As a result of their fear and search for a partner who does not exist, people reject perfectly healthy love relationships. You will not ever find a partner who can do everything that gives you a sense of security because if they have to travel far to be with you, they have to give up some of their independence. A good relationship cannot have a dynamic where one partner expects the other partner to automatically divulge information just to assuage their partner's insecurities.

Nobody can provide you with all you need to feel secure. Because texts are private, some couples might not want to show their partner every text they send or receive. However, this does not imply that the contents of such texts are untrustworthy. A request like that can result in your partner saying no, which can make the insecurely attached feel anxious. The problem is that there will always be a barrier, as seen in the text example, which prevents complete transparency. In that situation, having a robot that has been thoroughly developed to meet your needs is necessary for having the ideal partner. Interpersonal interactions require trust, so if you want anything to change, you must improve yourself. Asking your partner to accommodate your insecurities will not make them go away; it will only postpone the anxious feelings. You will not be able to go forward until you deal with the underlying causes of your problem.

You must begin becoming your main supporter if you want to change. Go within and acknowledge your responsibility for the status of your relationship before attempting to place the blame for how you feel on your partner. You will typically find that some relationship problems are a result of insecurity. Your partner likely has some accountability of their own, and some of your concerns may be valid, but when you do not even consider that you might be contributing to the issue, you are doing your relationship and yourself a big injustice. Encourage yourself to become more self-aware as you travel this path. Before your anxiety destroys a perfectly good relationship, figure out what makes you anxious.

Chapter 19:
Envisioning the Future

A secure attachment is attainable, but if you want to try to achieve it, you should be aware that it will not happen overnight. It is doable, but it does require some time and patience.

In the future, you will not even be aware that you are displaying traits of someone with a secure attachment style. It might not seem like this change is for the best, but it is.

The Traits of Someone With a Secure Attachment Style

The following are some of the traits that you might start displaying in the future:

1. You openly express your feelings.

You will feel at ease explaining how you genuinely feel and expressing your emotions. You do not try to hide your preferences or give in to peer pressure to adopt other people's ideas, values, or preferences. Also, you will not feel bad about yourself and will be able to handle any difficulties that may come your way. Speaking your views or confronting someone who is being impolite or improper will not make you terrified.

You will not always require someone to make you feel good or validate you. You trust your values and opinions and accept yourself. You will not be afraid to express your thoughts or stand up for what you believe in, even if those close to you do not agree with you or want the same things that you do. You will be able to tell what is important and worth protecting from what is merely amusing or not worth the effort. This is an excellent indication that your mind is growing the capacities required to sustain a joyful and healthy state of mind in the future.

2. You trust others.

You will be able to trust other people. You will not feel frightened, in danger, or uneasy with strangers. Even people you do not know well will reassure you that everything will be fine and make you feel safe. Because you are at ease with yourself and your surroundings, you will not feel awkward when you are around or meeting new people.

You may also rely on the fact that others will only follow you if they approve of the fact that your goals differ from theirs, especially if they are for the benefit of everyone. Even though this may entail opposing beliefs and ideals, you are confident in your ability to keep everyone safe and to have faith in others to do what is right.

3. You are independent.

You will experience independence. You do not have to be afraid of being alone, uncertain, or like you do not have enough to offer the world. If you do not want to feel alone in this world, you can ask for assistance when you need it.

You will not base your decisions or ideas on those of others. You can view situations from your vantage point and determine if they are best seen in their true context or not. To feel liked or accepted, you do not need anything or anyone else to do it for you. You do not need anyone's permission to recognize the good in anything or anyone. You may be yourself, concentrate on what you can do in this life, and be content with who you are and what you have.

4. You develop self-regulation.

Making decisions is possible without feeling overly anxious. Your mental health enables you to share your accountability with other people while also allowing you to take ownership of your mistakes and accept responsibility for your actions. You can also do this without feeling ashamed, or concerned about how other people would see you.

5. You are balanced and in control.

Overall, you will feel in charge of your life and at peace. Instead of being worried, pressured, or overburdened, you can make the most of your time, be productive, and feel at ease. You do not get overwhelmed easily, and it is simple for you to maintain present-moment awareness. This includes being aware of your own needs, desires, and values as well as those of others. You may accept individuals for who they are rather than strive to change or mold them into what you want them to be.

6. You are mature, realistic, and responsible.

You will be able to see your life and yourself. You are not a slave to your emotions; therefore, you may make decisions based on what is most significant or relevant as opposed to your sentiments of fear, rage, or guilt. You will be able to prioritize these feelings so they do not get in the way of what is going on in the moment or your life right now.

You will have confidence in your past and faith in your future. You will be able to view the world around you and make judgments based on it if you have a realistic understanding of how things work. You can ask questions rather than allow other people's explanations or assumptions to instill false hopes or expectations in your mind.

You will not need to worry about your emotions controlling your actions so you can lead a happy and fulfilling life. It could take some time to develop these skills, but the effort will be worthwhile in the end.

Conclusion

Although managing anxious attachment in relationships is not simple, it is doable. You need to have the patience and willingness to work on it. It is crucial that you never quit and give yourself enough time and space to improve. One way to maintain a strong bond is to have your partner's support. You will need to be patient and emotionally strong, so it will not be simple. You can overcome it, though, if your partner is understanding and supportive enough.

If you keep dealing with your anxious attachment, you might discover that your relationship is stronger than you anticipated. Work over your insecurities so that your relationship can develop rather than allowing them to stand in the way. You and your partner will be able to communicate more and share a stronger bond as a result of this new understanding.

In relationships, anxious attachment is a prevalent issue. It will make you act differently than your partner. You may find yourself feeling insecure or avoidant. It will cause you to act in ways that may hurt the relationship. But you may learn how to handle the problems by understanding this attachment style and how it impacts your relationships. You can strengthen your bond and discover techniques for avoiding uneasy attachment in the future.

Anxious attachment occurs when there is uncertainty about an attachment bond. There is a lack of trust and fear of losing the relationship. A relationship's insecurity or problems that make a person fear being rejected or abandoned may also contribute to it. One may become avoidant or exhibit jealous rage as a result of anxious attachment.

It is influenced by a wide range of factors, both internal and external. An anxious person sees the world differently than their partner does. Anxiety results from these perceptional discrepancies. When this occurs, the anxious partner may either cling to or distance themselves from others, which will harm the relationship.

Relationship anxiety can be managed, but it will take time and persistence. You will need to exercise patience if your partner is anxious since they can act in ways that are not best for your relationship. You must thus allow them the room and time they require to heal themselves. If you do this, there is a good chance that you can truly get through this together.

Both partners need to have a certain level of trust in the early stages of a relationship. You have to have faith that your partner will not hurt you or leave you. You must take the time to get to know one another to develop that trust. This may contribute to laying the groundwork for a stronger relationship later. You will be able to tell more clearly whether there are issues after spending some time getting to know one another. This will enable you to address any potential problems.

If you are dealing with someone who has an anxious attachment style, then you need to be willing to work on it. Occasionally, your partner could behave in a way that even they find surprising. This is because they may be insecure and terrified of losing you. When this occurs, they can become angry and act in a way they will later regret. It is essential that you love them enough to give them the room and time they require for healing. You must have patience and consider their situation.

I hope that this book helped you understand anxious attachment in relationships. Even though it may have been a bit alarming at first, you will be able to deal with it. There is no doubt that the greatest way to deal with anxious attachment is to have a partner who is prepared to work through your problems with you.

Author's Note

Dear reader,

I hope you enjoyed my book.

Please don't forget to toss up a quick review on amazon, I will personally read it! Positive or negative, I'm grateful for all feedback.

Reviews are so helpful for self-published authors and your feedback can make such a difference for my book!

Thanks very much for your time, and I look forward to hearing from you soon.

Sincerely,

Alison

Made in the USA
Las Vegas, NV
17 June 2023

73548060R00075